WESTMAR COLLE

DO RELIGIOUS CLAIMS MAKE SENSE?

An Essay in the Epistemology of Religion

DO
RELIGIOUS CLAIMS
MAKE SENSE?

STUART C. BROWN

THE MACMILLAN COMPANY
NEW YORK

© SCM Press Ltd 1969
Library of Congress Catalog Card No. 71–93568

Printed in Great Britain

CONTENTS

v

ABBREVIATIONS

APR   *An Analytical Philosophy of Religion* by W. F. Zuurdeeg, Nashville (Abingdon Press) and London (Allen & Unwin) 1959

CPR   *Critique of Pure Reason* (2nd Edition 1787) by Kant, tr. N. K. Smith, London (Macmillan) 1929

EC   *The Essence of Christianity* (2nd Edition 1843) by L. A. Feuerbach, tr. George Eliot, reprinted New York (Harper Torchbooks) 1957

EHU   *Enquiry concerning Human Understanding* (1777 edition) by Hume, ed. L. A. Selby-Bigge, Oxford (OUP) 1902

FK   *Faith and Knowledge* by John Hick, Ithaca, N.Y. (Cornell U.P.) and London (OUP) 1957

FP   *Faith and the Philosophers* edited by John Hick, London (Macmillan) and New York (St Martin's Press) 1964

LTL   *Language, Truth and Logic* by A. J. Ayer, London (Victor Gollancz) 2nd Edition 1946 and New York (Dover) 1946

KM   *Kerygma and Myth* edited by H.-W. Bartsch and translated by R. H. Fuller, London (SPCK) Vol. I 1953, Vol. II 1962

JCM   *Jesus Christ and Mythology* by Rudolf Bultmann, New York (Scribners) 1958 and London (SCM Press) 1960

RU   *Religion and Understanding* edited by D. Z. Phillips, Oxford (Blackwell) and New York (Macmillan) 1967

SMG   *The Secular Meaning of the Gospel* by Paul van Buren, New York (Macmillan) and London (SCM Press) 1963

ST   *Systematic Theology* by Paul Tillich, Chicago (University of Chicago Press) and London (Nisbet) Vol. I 1953

THN   *Treatise of Human Nature* by Hume, ed. L. A. Selby-Bigge, Oxford (OUP)

PREFACE

THIS ESSAY is concerned with a cluster of related problems which arise for an understanding of religious belief. In my treatment of them I have confined myself to examples drawn almost entirely from the Christian religion. I have accepted this restriction more out of necessity than partiality. It is difficult enough for a European philosopher to avoid unintentionally caricaturing that religion. The risk of his misrepresenting religions which have little influenced his own culture must be even greater. I have, however, tried to make a virtue out of this restriction by addressing myself to some issues which have been of particular concern to Christian thinkers in recent years. But I hope that the bearing of my treatment of them on religious belief in general will be apparent. For few of them are peculiar to the Christian religion.

The starting-point and central theme of this essay is the difficulty which people who do not profess to be in any way religious find in making sense of the practice of religion. Some are content to say that it is largely wishful thinking bolstered up by communal practices. But others, for one reason or another, do not find such an account satisfactory. Their difficulty is not so much that they consider religious claims to make excessive demands on the credulity. It is rather that they are unable to grasp at all firmly just what it is religious people believe. They are indeed unable to accept the claims of religion as true. But this is not because these claims seem to them to be manifestly false. It is rather because they are unable to grasp firmly what it would be like for these claims to be true. They may, or may not, be inclined to admit that religious "believers" are better placed than themselves. But, so far as they are concerned, the claims of religion are largely unintelligible.

I hope that such people will find some interest in the arguments to be found in this essay. But it should be stressed that it is no part of my purpose to make the claims of religion intelligible in non-religious terms. My central problem may indeed be identified in apologetic terms as "the problem of communication". But an epistemological treatment demands a less question-begging way of putting it. For some philosophers have provided what has been considered a *rationale* for supposing that there is nothing—at any rate by way of truth—for religion to communicate. The question needs to be answered: Do the claims of religion make sense? The problem should therefore be posed in more neutral terms.

It is for this reason that I pose the problem by saying that there is an *apparent* "intelligibility gap" between believer and non-believer. In particular there are claims the believer is inclined to make which do not quite make sense to the unbeliever. This situation has called forth a range of different explanations from both philosophers and theologians. I have reduced this range to seven different types of thesis which have, or might have, been put forward in this connection. These are listed in the scheme given of the argument immediately below. My discussion of these theses will be wholly philosophical. But I have thought it wrong to frustrate the interest of those who have little or no acquaintance with philosophy by taking such prior knowledge of the subject for granted. Accordingly I shall be at pains to explain such jargon as I have found it convenient to employ. I have also embodied in Chapter I something of an introduction to the kinds of epistemological question which provide a background to philosophical treatments of this apparent intelligibility gap.

In developing the ideas contained in this essay I have profited considerably from discussion with other philosophers. In particular, Gerald A. Cohen, David Hamlyn, Dewi Phillips, Keith Ward and Peter Winch have read and commented upon earlier versions. Christopher Olsen and Lloyd Reinhardt have discussed particular issues with me. I should like both to acknowledge my indebtedness to them and to absolve them from any responsibility for the errors the essay will no doubt be found to contain. I should like also to thank Mrs Susan Cunnew for her typing assistance. Finally I should like to record my gratitude to my wife, Mavis. She has been a constant source of help and encouragement at every stage.

Birkbeck College, London   S.C.B.
December, 1968

SCHEME OF THE ARGUMENT

A LARGE part of the structure of the reasoning presented in what follows may be indicated by reference to the apparent "intelligibility gap" by virtue of which the unbeliever is not able to attach sense to the claims of religion. For a number of theses have been advanced in which distinctive positions have been adopted with regard to it. Together with a view which I shall elaborate for the sake of completeness, they seem indeed to constitute the full range of positions in relation to which this apparent intelligibility gap may be characterized. They may now be listed:

1. *Religious claims simply are unintelligible.* I shall refer to theses of this kind as "*U-theses*".[1] Their account of the intelligibility gap presents it as *merely* apparent. On this view, the claims of religion do not make sense to the non-believer for the reason that they simply do not make sense. It follows from this that such claims do not make sense to the believer either. They may be of emotional significance to him, according to this account, but they cannot have "factual significance" for him.

U-theses assume that one can appeal to quite general standards of what it makes sense to say, standards which are binding upon all discourse. Philosophers have sometimes attempted to show that such an assumption is indeed a valid one. They have done this in three distinct, if sometimes inter-related ways. Their U-theses have sometimes been based on:

[1] I hope that readers will find this short-hand helpful. My reasons for adopting it are two-fold: (a) to avoid having to choose between a misleadingly brief or a repetitiously elaborate way of referring to these views: and, more importantly, (b) to help make clear when I am discussing one of these positions *as such* rather than some particular *version* of it. It will be apparent that the untenability of the U-thesis as such would not follow from the untenability of some particular version of it.

(*a*) considerations to do with human nature (I discuss this kind of support for such a thesis in Chapter II); (*b*) the claim that the possibility of significant discourse depends upon a correspondence between the structure of our language and the structure of the world; and (*c*) views advanced, e.g. by A. J. Ayer,[2] about the way in which the "meaningfulness" of a claim is decidable by considering in what way sense experience would be relevant to deciding whether or not it is true. I shall discuss versions (*b*) and (*c*) of the U-thesis in Chapter III.

2. *Religious claims are unintelligible as they stand but can be rendered intelligible by a particular re-interpretation of them.* I shall refer to theses of this kind as "*R-theses*" since the term "reductionist" is commonly applied to them. Like U-theses, they suppose there to be quite general standards of intelligibility to which all claims are subject. We can only make sense of religious claims, according to such an account, by reducing them to claims made in terms to which sense can be attached. But for the availability of such a re-interpretation of the claims of religion they would, it is said, have to be regarded as simply unintelligible. For they do not make sense as they stand. Perhaps the most sustained attempt to develop an R-thesis in relation to Christian belief is that made by L. A. Feuerbach.[3] I shall discuss the relevant aspects of his work in Chapter II.

3. *Religious claims have become unintelligible, as a result of conceptual change.* I shall refer to theses of this kind as "*C-theses*". Advocates of such a view concede that religious claims may at one time have been intelligible. The explanation of their not making sense to us may, on such an account,[4] be referred to changes in

[2] *Language, Truth and Logic*, London (Victor Gollancz) and New York (Dover) 1936. I shall refer to this work throughout as "LTL", giving a number which corresponds to the pagination of the Second (1946) Edition.

[3] *The Essence of Christianity* (2nd Edition 1843) tr. George Eliot, reprinted in the Harper Torchbook Series, New York, 1957. Hereinafter referred to as "EC".

[4] I discuss this view in connection with A. C. MacIntyre's paper "Is understanding religion compatible with believing?". It is published in *Faith and the Philosophers* (ed. J. Hick), London (Macmillan) 1964, hereinafter referred to as "FP". MacIntyre seems to rely on a C-thesis in this paper, though I do not think he would now wish to endorse such a thesis.

the pattern of life of the society to which we belong. Part and parcel with such social change is the loss of certain concepts which only had their place in the context provided by a way of life that has now passed into history. This is so, it is said, of religious concepts. We can, by careful and sympathetic study, do something to reconstruct in our imaginations something of that way of life. And by this means we may come to some understanding of the sense which religious concepts once had. But the terms on which this is possible preclude our coming to share these concepts. For they cannot hold their place in the context of a secularized society. The C-thesis will be discussed in Section 16.

4. *Religious claims have become unintelligible, as a result of conceptual change, but can be re-expressed in such a way that they can once more be understood.* I shall refer to theses of this kind as "*D-theses*", since the attempt so to express the claims of religion in a systematic way has come to be known as "demythologizing". It will be apparent that D-theses stand in the same relation to C-theses as R-theses stand to U-theses. The difference between the former kinds of thesis and the latter lies in the epistemological foundations on which they are respectively based. For C-theses and D-theses do presuppose, as do U-theses and R-theses, that there are universally valid standards of intelligibility. Their common epistemological assumption is that common standards of intelligibility do prevail throughout any given society at any given time. If such an assumption cannot be supported, neither a C-thesis nor a D-thesis will be tenable. But the D-thesis, like the R-thesis, faces problems of its own. In Chapter V, I shall consider Rudolf Bultmann's[5] form of D-thesis.

5. *Religious claims are not, strictly speaking, either "true" or "false", but are expressions of a non-factual "perspective" by which human life*

[5] See his *Jesus Christ and Mythology*, New York (Scribner's) 1958, London (SCM Press) 1960 and hereinafter referred to as "JCM". See also *Kerygma and Myth* (ed. H.-W. Bartsch, tr. R. H. Fuller), London (SPCK) Vol. I 1953, Vol. II 1962. Hereinafter referred to respectively as KM I and KM II.

may be lived. I shall refer to such theses as *"P-theses"*, since the term "perspective" is employed by Paul van Buren,[6] whose version I consider in Section 17. A P-thesis may be advanced on the same basis as a U-thesis. To some extent, indeed, van Buren does assume such a basis. But there are considerations which may be advanced to give independent support for a P-thesis. These derive, in particular, from the arguments which favour saying that any genuinely factual claim must (in principle) be falsifiable. This requirement is not met by a number of central religious affirmations. Van Buren is also influenced by the form of P-thesis suggested by R. M. Hare.[7] He wishes, that is to say, to give an account of religious affirmations which recognizes their failure to meet this requirement but which none the less accords some value to them. The requirement itself will be examined in Chapter VI.

6. *Religious beliefs are superstitious.* *"S-theses"*, as I shall call them, represent religious beliefs as subject to standards of what it makes sense to say which they fail to meet. An S-thesis is not infrequently put forward as a corollary to a U-thesis. As such, it would stand or fall with the form of U-thesis upon which it depends. What an S-thesis may add, in such cases, is an attempt to show that religious beliefs also fail to meet the standards of *rationality* to which they are subject in being subject to these standards of intelligibility. Those who claim that religious beliefs are simply the product of wishful thinking are usually committed to this form of S-thesis. A more subtle form of S-thesis is, however, available, which does not depend on the tenability of any form of U-thesis. For it may be possible, by careful examination of the method of reasoning employed in support of a given set of beliefs, to detect the standards by which they should be judged. It is unlikely that this form of S-thesis would license a *holus-bolus* dismissal of religious claims. For a great variety of reasons have been given in support of

[6] *The Secular Meaning of the Gospel*, London (SCM Press) and New York (Macmillan) 1963, hereinafter referred to as "SMG".
[7] *New Essays in Philosophical Theology* ed. Flew arn MacIntyre, London (SCM Press) and New York (Macmillan) 1955, p. 101f.

them. I know of no explicit attempt to develop such a thesis. Hume, in his *Dialogues concerning Natural Religion*, comes quite close to doing so against the hypothesis that the universe was created by an infinite intelligence. But his arguments bear on the claim *qua* hypothesis, i.e. on the claim as supported by the arguments of natural religion. But it cannot be claimed *a priori* that there could not be a basis for belief that the universe was created by an infinite intelligence against which Hume's arguments would not apply. Some examples will be given, in Chapter VII, of ways in which such an S-thesis might be developed.

7. *Religious beliefs are unintelligible to the unbeliever by virtue of his being an unbeliever.* This is the only account of the intelligibility gap which regards it as both a genuine and an essential feature of the situation between believer and unbeliever. Other theses, like the D-thesis and the P-thesis, which represent the gap as genuine, also claim that it can be eliminated. Some accounts which regard it as inevitable that the unbeliever should not be able to make sense of religious claims are, not surprisingly, only acceptable to a believer. This would be so when the gap is accounted for by saying that the unbeliever "lacks divine grace" and hence is not able to understand the claims of religion. But there are epistemological forms of this thesis which neither rule out nor entail a religiously biassed description of the situation. There is indeed one form of such a thesis which, in claiming belief to be a *condition* of understanding religion, gives it a distinctly apologetic slant.[8] But, as I shall indicate in Section 24, such an interpretation of the tenet *Nisi credideritis, non intelligetis* is not epistemologically viable.

There is indeed some reason to associate available forms of this thesis with apologetics. But the "*B-thesis*", as I shall call it, is itself epistemological. Its advocates have therefore tried to show its tenability in other areas than that of religion. This is true of Richardson and also of those forms of B-thesis presented

[8] For example, that advocated by Alan Richardson in *Christian Apologetics*, London (SCM Press) and New York (Harper & Row) 1947.

by J. Hick[9] and W. F. Zuurdeeg.[10] If one accepts such a thesis one must allow that the claims of religion may be intelligible to those who make them. But one is not thereby committed to conceding the truth of any religious claim. For the B-thesis is concerned primarily in contending the inseparability of belief and understanding with regard to certain kinds of statement. It is important to a plausible form of B-thesis that religion should not provide the only instances of this anomaly. I say it is an "anomaly" because it is apparent that, as far as concerns most of the statements we make, it seems in principle possible to understand them while withholding judgment as to their truth or falsity. If it is claimed that this is not so for all statements whatever, examples need to be given which are, at any rate, less contentious than religious examples would be. Hence a B-thesis with regard to religious claims has to be supported by a B-thesis with regard to a particular kind of claim not peculiar to religion.

I shall try to show that acceptance of a B-thesis is compatible with either (*a*) accepting religious claims as true or (*b*) regarding them as false. It has sometimes been held that if one regards religious claims as unintelligible or finds them unintelligible, it is not open to one to regard them as false. But I shall try to show that this need not be so. More controversially, the B-thesis precludes the possibility of a man's rejecting religious claims as *false* yet at the same time knowing what it would be like for them to be true.

The main scheme of argument in this essay will be directed towards establishing, first, the *probability*, and second, the *possibility*, of a B-thesis being tenable with regard to religious claims. This may seem the wrong way round, since one usually establishes or assumes that a thesis is possible *before* considering its probability. But I do not, in arguing that a B-thesis of some form is probably correct, presuppose that such a thesis is

---

[9] *Faith and Knowledge*, Ithaca N.Y. (Cornell U.P.) and London (OUP), Second Edition 1967. Hereinafter referred to as "FK".

[10] *An Analytical Philosophy of Religion*, Nashville (Abingdon Press) 1958 and London (Allen & Unwin) 1959, hereinafter referred to as "APR".

possible. For my argument is that it is as probable that some form of B-thesis is correct as it is improbable that any of the six other kinds of thesis can be sustained. For these seven theses do, it seems to me, exhaust the possible range of theses which can be contemplated in relation to the intelligibility gap. To the extent, therefore, that any six of them can confidently be eliminated as non-viable, we have reason for looking with particular care to see if any form of the seventh thesis will provide us with an acceptable account.

Some indication may be given as to why these seven theses should be thought to be the only possible rival kinds of thesis which can be considered in this connection. Firstly, we may divide theses about the nature of the intelligibility gap into those which take religious claims as purporting to make claims of fact and those which construe such claims as neither "true" nor "false". If a P-thesis is untenable, then religious claims have to be taken as *purporting* to say something about what is the case. But now, given that the unbeliever finds such claims unintelligible, this must be either because they *are* unintelligible or because they are for some reason so *to him*. To show that they are unintelligible we need to appeal to standards of what it makes sense to say. They must clearly be standards to which religious claims are subject. And they seem to be of three kinds: (*a*) quite general standards; (*b*) standards which govern discourse in a given culture; and (*c*) standards to which religious claims can, by the way they are supported, be shown to be subject. If (*a*) or (*b*) were thought correct, it might still be held that the claims of religion could be made intelligible. But if not, then D-theses and R-theses, as well as C-theses and U-theses, would be untenable. Unless, therefore, it is possible to establish (*c*), it seems as if it must be concluded that some form of B-thesis is correct. For it seems as if no alternative would remain to us except to say that it has—for some reason—to do with the unbeliever not being a believer that he does not find the claims of religion intelligible.

One reason why I have given priority to establishing the

probability of some form of B-thesis being correct in this connection is that many—like myself—may only be forced to consider
the *possibility* that such an account may be correct by being
unable to accept any of the alternative positions. This is not
just a matter of prejudices about religion. There are also a
number of well-established philosophical tenets which seem
to rule out a viable form of B-thesis. In arguing for the *possibility*
of a B-thesis, therefore, I shall be attempting to create the
epistemological space within which it might be advanced. To
do this, I shall be concerned to displace those orthodoxies in
some measure. Thus, in Chapter IV, I shall argue that the
widely held view which makes necessary truth depend wholly
upon conventions regarding our symbolism cannot adequately
account for conceptual change. In Chapter VI, I shall try to
show that it cannot be an absolutely general requirement of a
claim's being "true" or "false" that something should be
counted as tending to falsify it. Since I am not concerned to
make a special case for religious claims, my arguments will have
implications for philosophical accounts of other claims, e.g.
some of those made in science.

A philosophical attempt to deal with the question whether
the claims of religion make sense is bound to be concerned
with the epistemological issues and their bearing upon religion.
Other aspects of the philosophy of religion enter into this essay
only marginally. In the final two chapters I relate my answer
to the question to two issues on which it has a bearing. The
first of these is the question of the status of the claim "God
exists" and in what sense, if any, it should be regarded as
necessarily true in the context of a given religion. The second
issue concerns the relation between the language of religion
and that of common life. One implication of a B-thesis will be
that, even if religious claims must be expressed in terms drawn
from the language of common life, they could never be made
wholly intelligible in those terms.

I

EPISTEMOLOGICAL BACKGROUND

THE ATTEMPT to outline the scope of human knowledge has formed a not inconsiderable part of that branch of philosophical inquiry known as "epistemology". Such a concern may strike the layman as at once presumptuous and misguided —presumptuous, because philosophers do not often even pretend to be particularly well-informed about the present state of scientific knowledge, and misguided because, even if they were, they would still be in no position to anticipate what limits may be set on its future development. But, on closer inspection, he will find that those who have engaged in such inquiries have not pretended either to omniscience or to an easy foresight. They have not, that is to say, been concerned with predicting how much their descendants would *in fact* be able to find out about the universe. The object of their inquiries, on the contrary, has been to determine how much could *in principle* be known. They will readily concede, therefore, that epistemology provides no crystal ball for looking into the future. Even a tentative prediction of what scientists will know in a few years' time could only be made by someone intimately acquainted with the relevant branch of scientific inquiry.

What, then, is there left for the epistemologist to do? What, that is to say, is the force of the distinction between what can *in fact* be known and what could *in principle* be known? Epistemologists have drawn this distinction in different terms. They have agreed, negatively, that it could not be a matter for empirical inquiry to determine what limits must be drawn to what can *in principle* be known of the universe. Such a matter would have to be decided independently of experience. But to say this is scarcely even to elaborate the distinction which is in question. What is needed is an account of the problematic half of the distinction.

One way of giving such an account is to say that any matter regarding which no one could hope to arrive at any understanding would be such as not to admit *in principle* of knowledge. For if no man could *understand* what it was for a given claim to be true, it would follow that no one could be said to *know* it to be true. It may be possible for *some* people to know something to be true even though they find it unintelligible. But this possibility requires there to be others, on whose authority the claim is accepted as true, who *do* understand the claim in question. Otherwise we should have to say that the words uttered do not constitute a claim *at all*. Nor should we be impressed by the fact that these words may be uttered in just the tone of voice appropriate to making a claim. For how could there be a *claim* which no one could understand?

If, then, one attempts to set the limits of human *knowledge*, this may be done by setting the limits of human *understanding*. The limits of what can *in principle* be known are the limits of what it makes sense to say. In a way, therefore, the epistemological inquiry into the limits of human knowledge is equally an inquiry into the limits of human ignorance. It is true that epistemologists have traditionally spoken as though there were certain matters regarding which human beings, owing to "the frailty of their faculties", must *necessarily* remain ignorant. But if this "necessary ignorance" is to do with what cannot intelligibly be said, it will not be possible to *state* what it is we can only be ignorant of. To that extent, it is no more possible for us to confess ignorance of those matters which lie outside human understanding than it is for us to claim knowledge of them.

But how could one justify saying that *no one* can make sense of a putative claim? How, in other words, can one tell that what sounds like a claim may, however the speaker may feel about it, fail actually to be one? The answer has been that certain conditions must be satisfied if what we say—or for that matter what we believe—is to make sense. These conditions have to do with what language must be like if discourse is to be possible. Any putative claim which fails to satisfy such conditions may be dismissed as a non-genuine one. But what are those conditions? This question takes us immediately into epistemological controversy. We can only answer it by looking at particular answers to it. No generally-negotiated answer has yet prevailed.

I. MEANING AND THE LIMITS OF HUMAN KNOWLEDGE

What conditions must be met if what is said is to make sense? One kind of answer to this question, which has commended itself in various forms to empiricists, has been given in terms of the relation which must hold between language and experience. A classical form of empiricist answer has been that all our ideas arise out of experience. The words we use, according to this view, acquired their meaning only through having become attached to ideas. Words like "red", "rough" and "round" stand for the ideas which we have of certain simple perceptible qualities. Such qualities clearly lie within the scope of human experience and therefore also of human understanding. The same is true of collections of such qualities, such as those to which we apply the words "table", "horse" and "hill". It is, moreover, possible for us to combine such qualities in our imaginations in such a way as to form ideas of fictitious entities. But such composite ideas are quite possible. The words which refer to them—such as "unicorn" and "golden mountain"—are therefore meaningful. Golden mountains and unicorns do not actually exist. But it is quite possible for us to engage in intelligible discourse about them. To that extent they may be said to lie within the scope of human knowledge.

It is in this empiricist spirit that Berkeley adopted his principle that *to be is to be perceived*.[1] For he wished to claim not

[1] *Principles of Human Knowledge*, Sect. 3ff. For a proper understanding of Berkeley's philosophy, it is important to bear in mind that he does not apply this principle to spirits and therefore not to talk about God. His *esse est percipi* principle is qualified, accordingly, by the addition of the clause

merely that there are, *as a matter of fact*, no existents which are not perceived but that it would *make no sense* to speak as if there were. Yet this is just the way in which Locke, according to Berkeley, was committed to speaking in his treatment of 'material substance'.

Locke himself had admitted that material substances as such were not available for perceptual inspection. Indeed, not merely were they not *in fact* observable, they were not the kind of thing which could *in principle* be perceived. To have said that they were not *in fact* observable is misleading in so far as it suggests—what Locke would have wished to deny—that material substances are fictitious entities like, say, unicorns. But unicorns, though they do not actually qualify for inclusion in any list of the kinds of thing there are in the world, are *in principle* observable. We should, that is to say, have no difficulty in understanding someone who claimed to have seen one nor indeed would we have much difficulty in identifying one if we were (*per improbabile*) to encounter one ourselves. But the position is quite different in this respect with material substances. For it is agreed both by Locke (who said there *were* such substances) and Berkeley (who said there were *not*) that there could be no question of anyone seeing a material substance. Someone who claimed to have seen one would not merely be mistaken in point of fact. He would betray a misunderstanding of the concept 'material substance'. For it belongs to the concept of material substance to which Berkeley denied any significant application that such substances lie outside the field of possible experience.

There is some analogy between the pattern of reasoning produced on each side of this dispute and that commonly produced in dispute about the existence of God. In each case it is agreed on both sides that the issue will not be settled by looking to see whether there is a phenomenon answering a given description. It is agreed, that is to say, that the issue is

---

"*aut percipere*". The point of this qualifying clause is precisely to legitimize significant talk about spirits as "existents". But this complication does not affect the argument here.

not an empirical one. It is, moreover, true that in each dispute one party has been inclined to press for something like a *necessary existence*, whereas the sceptical party has tended to claim that it does not even make sense to speak of such an existence. The analogy may indeed be taken further. For there is a remarkable similarity between the arguments used by Locke to support his claim that material substances exist and those used by Berkeley in favour of holding that God exists. Locke wishes to say that we cannot give an intelligible account of sense-perception without admitting the existence of material substances. And Berkeley argues that for the very same reason we must admit the existence of an omnipresent spirit whom we call "God". They both agree that, when our simple ideas of sense (or perceptions) are veridical, they must have been brought about in us by something independent of ourselves. On Locke's view, the power to produce such perceptions in us resides in material substances, which therefore must be supposed to exist. On Berkeley's view, it is God who is responsible for these veridical ideas. Each tries to show that nothing else than the kind of existence for which they are contending will suffice to make sense of our having non-delusive experiences at all.

Locke's account[2] is presented largely in traditional terms. He speaks of the difficulty in imagining "how these simple ideas can subsist by themselves". It is on account of this difficulty that, he suggests, "we accustom ourselves to suppose some *substratum* wherein they do subsist, and from which they do result, which therefore we call *substance*". It is evident from this kind of remark that Locke's attention has been attracted to the etymological aspect of the word "substance". He speaks of substance as that which "supports", "upholds" or "under-props" qualities. But the weight of his argument for material substances seems to fall elsewhere.

When our senses are not deceiving us, he argues, our simple ideas appear to be "the effect of powers in things without us". What he calls "qualities" are simply such powers to produce ideas in us. But powers cannot exist without belonging to

[2] *Essay concerning Human Understanding*, Bk. II, Ch. XXIII.

something which could be said to "have" them. Consequently, material substances, as those things to which such powers are ascribed, must exist. Not all qualities of bodies are, on Locke's view, of the same kind. Some, known as "secondary qualities", produce ideas of sense in us which bear no resemblance to properties belonging to the bodies themselves. Such qualities include colour, taste and sound. The ideas produced in us by such secondary qualities might be very different were our perceptual faculties different. Other qualities, known as "primary qualities", may be said to "really exist in the bodies themselves". These include those which produce in us ideas of extension, solidity, figure, motion and number. The ideas produced in us do not equally inform us of the nature of the bodies from which they originate. But we can only make sense of them as ideas *not originating in ourselves* by supposing that even those which do not so inform us originate in some way from those bodies.

Locke's account is, however, commonly thought[3] to make the concession that material bodies or substances are not, in principle, directly accessible to the senses. And this is, for Berkeley, enough to warrant excluding talk about "material substances" as meaningless. In insisting that it makes no sense to speak of anything (except a spirit) existing which is not actually being perceived, he adopts a "positivist" position (or what I call a U-thesis) about such supposed entities.

It should be stressed, however, that Berkeley's argument does not rest solely on a doctrinaire appeal to his *esse est percipi* principle. For, in a sense, the whole of his *Principles* is devoted to a justification of that principle. He is concerned to give an account of sense-experience which does not require there to be inobservables to make such experience intelligible. His argument is thus designed to solve the Lockean problem in non-Lockean terms. Thus his claim that the idea of material

[3] A. D. Woozley, in his Introduction to the Fontana Edition of Locke's *Essay*, has given reason for doubting whether this orthodox (Berkeleyan) interpretation is correct. But since I am here concerned with the issue Berkeley takes with him, Berkeley's "Locke" will suffice for present purposes.

substance is redundant is of greater philosophical import than his claim that it is meaningless or self-contradictory. For it provides the needed justification for the terms in which he dismisses the idea of material substance as meaningless or self-contradictory. Thus he claims, in reply to the allegation that his account of sense-experience destroys "the whole corpuscular philosophy" by abandoning the idea of material substance, that: "There is not any one *phaenomenon* explain'd on that supposition which may not as well be explain'd without it" (Sect. 50). Indeed, he elsewhere claims, to suppose that there are such substances is "to suppose, without any reason at all, that God has created innumerable beings that are entirely useless, and serve to no manner of purpose" (Sect. 19).

We have no need, on Berkeley's account, of 'material substance' in order to make sense of our experience. But, it turns out, we do not need it precisely because our need for something outside of ourselves to be the cause of our veridical perceptions is met elsewhere. It seems to be a premiss of Berkeley's reasoning that only what is active can be a cause. Given this premiss, he is able to argue that "matter is said to be passive and inert, and so cannot be an agent or efficient cause" (Sect. 69). But now if (*a*) we can only make intelligible to ourselves our having veridical perceptions by supposing them to be brought about by something independent of ourselves; and if (*b*) a cause must, as Berkeley thought, be an agent; it follows that "the cause of ideas is an incorporeal, active substance or spirit" (Sect. 26). And since no ordinary spirit could bring about our veridical ideas of sense in us, it follows that the existence of God is a condition[4] of our making sense of our having veridical ideas of sense. Berkeley shares premiss (*a*) with Locke. But premiss (*b*) has commended itself to no other philosopher of consequence.

What is noteworthy about this argument, apart from its sheer implausibility, is that it would have shown, if correct, that no purely secular conceptual scheme would be adequate to make sense of ordinary veridical sense-experience. For a

---

[4] I shall discuss Berkeley's presentation of this argument for the existence of God in Section 27 below.

purely secular conceptual scheme does not provide for the
kind of incorporeal spirit to which we must, on Berkeley's
argument, refer as the cause of those ideas which we do bring
about in ourselves. Materialism, according to Berkeley, is not
anti-religious because it is empirically-inclined. It is so only
because it is not sufficiently empirical. On Berkeley's view[5], a
truly radical empiricism was not merely compatible with, but
actually required the existence of a God.

Berkeley's "positivism" led him to give an alternative account
of Locke's problem. But he might be criticized on the ground
that the terms in which he rejects 'material substance' betray
his failure to understand the notion. This is the kind of charge
to which any positivist position may seem to be open. One way
of anticipating and obviating this charge is to turn reductionist.
For the reductionist is committed to claim, not merely that he
understands a given kind of claim, but that he understands
it better than those who put it forward. What they *purport* to
say, he will argue, does not make sense as it stands. Yet some
meaning, if not the one intended, can be attached to what is
said. This is indeed the *only* meaning that could be attached to
what is said. It is, therefore, what must *really* be meant by the
kind of claim in question.

2. THE PARADOX OF REDUCTIONISM

A good example of reductionist argument is to be found in
Hume's treatment of the idea of 'necessary connection'. Hume
draws attention[6] to the obscurity of the ideas of 'power',
'force', 'energy' and 'necessary connection'. He states his
intention of trying "to fix, if possible, the precise meaning of
these terms". Elsewhere,[7] he notes that these terms (and

---

[5] In this respect, Berkeley's position is close to that of Leibniz. I discuss
one aspect of Leibniz' combination of radical empiricism and a religious
metaphysic in Section 10.

[6] *Enquiry concerning Human Understanding*, Sect. VII, Pt. I, hereinafter
referred to as "EHU". Page references will be to the OUP edition by
Selby-Bigge.

[7] *Treatise on Human Nature*, Bk. I, Pt. 3, Sect. XIV, hereinafter referred
to as "THN". Page references will be to the OUP edition by Selby-Bigge.

here h eincludes "efficacy", "agency" and "productive quality") are "all nearly synonymous" and that, therefore, "it is an absurdity to employ any of them in defining the rest".

To define a word in terms of its synonyms is, for Hume, "absurd" because such a procedure does not bring us any nearer to the sense-impressions from which the underlying idea is derived. Words, for him, mean the ideas they stand for. If there is no idea corresponding to a given impression, that impression must be meaningless. Ideas in turn represent impressions gained through the senses or from the mind reflecting upon itself. As Hume puts it:

> all our ideas are nothing but copies of impressions . . . . in other words . . . . it is impossible for us to *think* of anything which we have not antecedently *felt*, either by our external or internal senses (EHU 62).

Hume searches, without success, for the source of the ideas of 'power' or 'necessary connection' among the impressions of the external senses. He notes that no contradiction would be involved in denying that an event, accepted as the "cause" of some other event, would be followed by that other event on some occasion of its occurrence. The connection which is said to hold between such events cannot, therefore, be a *logical* necessity. Yet what other kind of necessary connection could there be? Hume is almost prepared to draw the positivist conclusion that it makes no sense to speak of "necessity" at all in this context:

> All events seem entirely loose and separate. One event follows another; but we never observe any tie between them. They seem *conjoined*, but never *connected*. And as we can have no idea of anything which never appeared to our outward sense or inward sentiment, the necessary conclusion *seems* to be that we have no idea of connection or power at all, and that these words are absolutely without meaning (EHU 74).

But not all avenues have yet been explored. Hume stands firmly by his claim, for which he is justly noted, that we can have no idea of necessary connection as holding between objects or events. The idea cannot, that is to say, be derived from any *external* impression. But the possibility remains open that this idea might be derived from an *internal* impresssion. This possibility is initially discounted, since it would involve attaching a meaning to talk about necessary connection which is very different from that intended. But once it is admitted, Hume has little difficulty in finding a source for the ideas of power or necessary connection:

> The mind is carried by habit, upon the appearance of one event, to expect its usual attendant, and to believe that it will exist. This connection, therefore, which we *feel* in the mind, this customary transition of the imagination from one object to its usual attendant, is the sentiment or impression from which we form the idea of power or necessary connection. Nothing farther is the case (EHU 75).

Hume thus offers two definitions of "cause". (1) He defines it as a "philosophical relation" (i.e. as a relation between objects or events) as "an object, followed by another, and where all the objects similar to the first are followed by objects similar to the second". (EHU 76) This is a positivist definition, since no idea of 'necessary connection' is admitted here at all, but only a constant conjunction between the events or objects. But (2) he also defines "cause" as a "natural relation", i.e. as a relation between ideas. So defined, it is "an object, followed by another, and whose appearance always conveys the thought to that other". (EHU 76) This is a reductionist definition, the necessary connection being located in the imagination as between ideas rather than in the world as between objects. In offering this second definition, Hume goes beyond a positivist thesis about natural necessity without in any way going back on it. He does so partly to show what *must* be meant by those who have spoken of necessary connections between events. But he is also trying to bring out the mistake involved in supposing that there are such connections *between events*. It is due, he says, to a propensity of the human mind "to spread itself on external objects, and to conjoin with them any internal impressions which they occasion". What has happened is that the repeated experience of particular chains of events leads us to feel a kind of necessity about the sequence, a necessity which we erroneously project on to the sequence itself. The result is that what we say does not, as it stands, make sense. To understand what sense can be attached to it is also to see why it is a mistake to attach the sense traditionally given to it.

It will now appear that there is something very paradoxical about Hume's reduction of natural necessity to a felt transition of the mind under certain conditions. For, on Hume's account, the traditional sense is not a sense at all. It is, it seems, a nonsensical sense. But if this is how Hume's view needs to be described, it suggests the following paradox. Hume wishes to claim *both* that it makes no sense to speak of necessary connections between events *and* that (nevertheless) he is in a position to say what those who have so spoken really meant. But it would seem to follow from its making no sense to speak of such natural necessity that Hume can make no sense of such talk. And, if he cannot, how could he be in a position to say what such talk really means? On the other hand, if he *is* in a position to say what such talk really means, he must understand it. And if he understands it, how can he say it is meaningless?

There is a difficulty here about Hume's account of meaning, on which his reduction is based. For either that account is adequate or it is not. If it is adequate, then either the expression "necessary connection" may be used meaningfully of the relation between events, or it may not, according to Hume's theory. If it may not, then that seems all Hume can say about the matter. If, on the other hand, it is not, then talk of natural necessity is not ruled out. Hume somehow wants to have it both ways, *both* to dismiss such necessity *and* to say what it really consists in. But to do this, he needs an intuitive grasp of what is meant by those who have spoken of necessary connections between events. And this is only possible for him if he is not bound in his understanding by his own account of meaning. But either he is inconsistent in doing this or, more probably, his account of meaning is inadequate.

There seems to be a paradox in any form of reductionism of the kind Hume puts forward with regard to 'necessary connection'. In order to be in a position to say what such an expression really means, one must presumably be able to attach sense to it. But the starting-point of the argument was that the expression in question was devoid of meaning. By denying independent meaning to an expression, the reductionist is committed to saying that it cannot be synonymous with any expression deemed meaningful by his account of meaning. But, in precisely the same sense of "meaning", he must also, *qua* reductionist, go on to claim that the expression in question *is* synonymous with some expression favoured by his own theory. It is not possible to have it both ways. Only a conflict between the reductionist's "official" account of meaning and what he actually finds meaningful can make such a possibility an apparent one.

Hume's difficulty results in part from his taking the word or expression as the basic unit of meaning. This leads him to neglect certain aspects of meaning which become more apparent when the emphasis is placed on the way words and expressions occur in making assertions, asking questions, giving orders, stating claims, and so on. He is led into an account of meaning which is at some points excessively stringent and at others downright lax. The difficulties of giving a Humean account of the meaning of such words as "not" and "or" need hardly to be pointed out. What is, perhaps, less obvious is that Hume's atomistic account of meaning commits him to an excessively liberal account of compound expressions. For they, on his principles, will be meaningful given only that their components are meaningful. Thus Hume allows: "A virtuous horse we can conceive; because, from our own feeling, we can conceive virtue; and this we may unite to the figure and shape of a horse, which is an animal familiar to us." (EHU 19) But, by making this concession, Hume is already indicating the laxity of his account of meaning. For, despite the respectable origins of our ideas of 'horse' and 'virtue', it is by no means clear that it does make sense to speak of a horse as "virtuous". There is, of course, no difficulty in thinking of a horse as well-trained or good-natured. But it is far from clear what it would be for a horse to behave virtuously, e.g. to act out of a sense of duty.

And, if this should seem primarily a criticism of Hume's account of virtue, it should be pointed out that matters do not stop here. On Hume's terms, nothing prevents us from speaking of virtuous houses or mountains.

3. MEANING AND INTELLIGIBILITY

Hume might have avoided these difficulties had he distinguished between the meaning of words or expressions, on the one hand, and that of assertions, questions and orders, on the other. One can be said to know the meaning of a word or expression if one knows how to use it in making assertions, asking questions, and so on. But to say this is to say, in opposition to Hume, that it is assertions, questions, and so on that are the primary units of meaning, not words and expressions. One indication that this is so is that it is difficult to say what it is to know the meaning of an assertion without being involved in circularity. Consider, for example, Wittgenstein's remark: "To understand a proposition means to know what is the case, if it is true." (*Tractatus Logico-Philosophicus*, 4.024) When one remembers that there is no difference between understanding what someone is claiming and knowing what he is claiming, such a remark may be paraphrased in such a way as to bring out this circularity: "To understand what someone is claiming is to know what would be the case, if what is claimed were true." The circularity is avoided in the account that can be given of what it is to understand an order. For an order may always be distinguished from its execution. Hence one can say that one understands an order if one knows what would count as carrying it out. But there is not an analogous distinction between a claim and what is the case if it is true. For to describe what is the case if it is true is to describe what is being claimed.

The distinction between the meaning of words or expressions, on the one hand, and assertions, questions and orders, on the other, may more readily be explained in what may appear to be an atomistic way. A word has meaning, it has been said, if it may be used in making claims, asking questions, and so on.

But it is quite possible to talk nonsense using only words which are themselves meaningful, e.g. "Necessity is in bed". This is possible only because in such a case there is a breach of the rules which implicitly govern the use of the words in question. Philosophers have been tempted to account for this kind of nonsense by saying that a "category-mistake" is involved. The concept 'necessity' is not in the same category as 'maiden aunt', 'a large kipper', and so on. Necessity is, to put it obscurely, *not the sort of thing* that could be "in bed". But there is some difficulty in dividing into categories without relying on what we are trying to clarify, namely, our intuitive grasp of what it makes sense to say and what not. In any case not all nonsense can be described in this way, as will shortly be seen.

It is possible for someone to have a somewhat formal grasp of the rules which govern the use of a particular expression such that he will not make the kinds of mistake which would betray a gross misunderstanding of it. Such a formal grasp of how to use an expression is, however, quite compatible with failing to find claims involving it intelligible.[8] Indeed, some such grasp of how to use an expression is required if one is able to say that some use of it is unintelligible. One needs, in other words, some capacity to *exercise* a concept in order to recognize that a given *application* of it cannot intelligibly be made.

This point was clearly recognized by Kant,[9] who was concerned to show how metaphysical disputes resulted from attempting to misapply certain concepts. There were, he thought, certain concepts which were indispensable to our thought about the world. Since they had therefore a pervasive character, there was a constant temptation to apply them in a

[8] I use "intelligible" throughout interchangeably with "fully intelligible" and "unintelligible" interchangeably with "not fully intelligible". I do this, since there is little philosophical interest in what is "fully *un*intelligible". Those who have denied the intelligibility of religious claims, e.g. "God is the Father of all mankind" have not wished to suggest that their status is that of gibberish.

[9] In his *Critique of Pure Reason* (2nd Ed. 1787) tr. N. Kemp Smith, London (Macmillan) 1929. Hereinafter referred to as "CPR".

wholly non-empirical way, to suppose indeed that they could provide us with metaphysical truth. There was, for example, a proof of the immortality of the soul which began from the premiss that the soul is a simple substance. This premiss, according to Kant, involves a misuse of the concept 'substance'. It is not that no sense at all can be attached to talk of the soul as a substance. On the contrary, it is precisely because *some* sense can be attached to it that those who engage in such talk are so easily persuaded that they have gained insight into a supra-sensible reality. But the concept 'substance' only has "objective meaning", on Kant's view, when applied to the objects of sense-experience, to what is spatial in character. Only when so applied could the claim that something is a substance be understood. Those who have supposed it might be possible to apply the concept 'substance' outside the field of possible sense-experience have been "palming off upon us what is a mere pretence of new insight" (CPR, A 350).

The distinction between being able to *exercise* a given concept and being prepared to *apply* it may be used to articulate a form of reductionism which is not vitiated by the paradox mentioned in the previous section. It is possible by this means to re-formulate Hume's thesis about 'necessary connection'. Instead of saying "What is said here is nonsense, but what is really meant must be . . .", an R-thesis might take the form: "What is said here is unintelligible, but what can and should have been said is . . .". Neglecting Hume's account of meaning, such a reformulation might be presented in the following terms:

We could claim that there are necessary connections between events *only* if *either* it involved a contradiction to assert
that one event will take place yet not one of a kind which
customarily attends it: *or* if such necessary connections
between events could themselves be observed. But neither of
these conditions obtains. Hence we cannot intelligibly speak
of *necessary*, nor therefore of *causal connections*, between events.
We can, however, attach some sense to what people say when
they claim that there are such connections. And this is how

we can see that they are wrong, indeed mistaken, in supposing there are. For there is application for *a* notion of 'necessary connection' in those very contexts. But this notion can
only be intelligibly applied to how we *feel* with regard to
those events, not to the events as such.

This form of R-thesis avoids Hume's mistake of supposing
that there can only be one true meaning of the expression
"necessary connection". It does not, therefore, presume to say
that what was really meant must have been different from
what was intended. Rather it is suggested that an unintelligible
claim has resulted from a confusion. In sorting out the confusion, the reductionist is able to point out what ought actually
to have been claimed.

The distinction between *exercising* a concept and *applying* it
is of some consequence for the argument of this essay. For if
it can be maintained, it will not follow from the fact that
religious (or any other) discourse is rule-governed that religious
claims are intelligible. Nor can what I have called the "intelligibility gap" be bridged by simply teaching the unbeliever
how religious vocabulary is used. For, if such a distinction be
admitted, it may be possible for someone to acquire a formal
grasp of religious language (by, for example, studying theology)
without finding religious claims intelligible. A man might, for
example, learn something of the kinds of action said to be "in
accordance with the will of God" without knowing what it is
to say this of them.

A convenient example is provided by Alasdair MacIntyre. He
wishes to oppose the suggestion that "agreement in following a
rule is sufficient to guarantee making sense" (FP 122). Against
this suggestion, he cites the word "taboo" as a case of a word
which has, he thinks, a clear enough use yet lacks sense:

> To call something taboo is not to prohibit it, but it is to say that it
> is prohibited. To say that something is taboo is to distinguish it
> from actions which are prohibited but are not taboo. We could say
> that it is to give a reason for a prohibition, except that it is un-
> intelligible what reason can be intended. So some theorists have
> constructed from the uses of taboo a sense which it might once
> have had and a possible history of how that sense was lost. *One*

cannot take the sense from the use, for the use affords no sense. (FP 122, italics mine)

MacIntyre cannot mean exactly what he says in claiming that the use of the word "taboo" affords "no sense". For, if that were so, he could not give *any* account of the word whatever. His point must therefore be that some grasp of the rules governing the use of the word "taboo" does not provide one with an ability to grasp what is being said of an action when it is said to *be* taboo. This is not to say, presumably, that one cannot have *some* understanding of what is being claimed, e.g. that the action is prohibited in an unusual way.

Another example of a concept which one may use without being able to apply to particular cases is that of 'Fate'. We have a number of expressions in current use embodying the word "Fate". It is often said, for example, that Fate "took a hand" or "intervened" on a given occasion. Most commonly of course this is no more than a slightly fanciful way of alluding to the unexpectedness (or perhaps fortuitous character) of some turn of events. But it would not have this use as a manner of speaking if nobody had ever believed that there was such an agency which did on occasion intervene in human affairs. We could indeed attach *some* sense to what was being said if someone actually claimed as much. Of course we *might* be mistaken in attaching the sense we do attach to it. We might wrongly expect the claim to be withdrawn for a given case when it transpires that what was taken to involve the hand of Fate is in fact the result of human conspiracy. But we *might* be right in expecting this. Indeed those who have claimed to believe in a Fate which intervened in human affairs have commonly confined themselves to matters over which human control was not possible. They have, that is to say, committed themselves, in claiming that some event is due to the intervention of Fate, to ruling out its being the result of human effort. One can understand this much about Fate without finding such talk intelligible. It is quite compatible with talk about Fate being rule-governed that it should not be found intelligible by anyone.

This example also illustrates a point which bears on the status of religious assertions. For it is quite consistent to maintain both that talk about Fate is *unintelligible* and that claims about the intervention of Fate may be *false*. If, for example, one knows that a given event was brought about by human contrivance one may claim that it would be false to say that it came about through the intervention of Fate. But, in claiming this, one is not conceding more than such partial intelligibility to this claim as is involved in its being subject to *any* rules. In distinguishing, therefore, between a rule-governed exercise of a concept and an intelligible application of it, we allow someone both to be an atheist and to deny the intelligibility of religious discourse. A man's rejection of religion might, that is to say, consist both in his holding beliefs which are incompatible with religious beliefs and in his regarding the claims of the believer as unintelligible. His so regarding them involves his not knowing what it would be for such claims to be true. He might, nevertheless, know what it would be for them to be false.

One immediate purpose of drawing the distinction between exercising a concept and applying it has been to suggest that there could be a form of R-thesis which is not vitiated by the paradox mentioned in the previous section. The ground is thus prepared for a form of reductionist thesis with regard to religious claims. A large part of the following chapter will be concerned with what is perhaps the most sustained attempt to develop such a thesis. It was made by Ludwig Feuerbach in his programme for reducing theology to what he called "anthropology".

II

RELIGION AND HUMAN NATURE

IT HAS already been indicated how reductionist (or R-) theses and positivist (or U-) theses may be connected. In particular, it has been seen how they both require an account of meaning which precludes the intelligibility of some discourse. Another way of putting this is to say that both need to establish or presuppose as universally valid certain standards of intelligibility. It is thus a necessary condition of a U-thesis or R-thesis being tenable with regard to religious claims that they can be shown to fall short of such standards.

It is of some importance for advocates of such theses to show that there are such quite general standards by which all discourse is to be judged. One argument of this esssay will be that, with certain qualifications, it neither has been nor can be shown that there are such quite general standards of what it makes sense to say. There have been three main sources from which philosophers have sought to derive such standards: (1) from considerations about human nature; (2) from theses about the relation which must obtain between language and reality; and (3) from considerations about the relevance which experience must have to significant inquiry. These will here be considered separately, though in practice they have often been related to one another in various ways.

Consideration of (2) and (3) will be given in the next chapter. The present chapter will be concerned with (1). Theses about human nature have commonly been designed to bring out what were thought to be necessary limitations in human capacity to understand the world. These limitations have been thought to derive from men being the kind of creatures they are. An interesting attempt to advance such a thesis was made by Feuerbach in his book *The Essence of Christianity*.

4. FEUERBACH'S REDUCTION OF THEOLOGY TO "ANTHROPOLOGY"

The distinction between exercising a concept and being able to apply it is of some importance for an understanding of Feuerbach's treatment of religion. Despite his claim that his work "contains a faithful, correct translation of the Christian religion out of the Oriental language of imagery into plain speech" (EC xxxiii), it is clear that what he goes on to offer is not strictly a *translation* at all. For his distinction between the "true meaning" and the "false meaning" of Christianity is a distinction between the sense which can and ought to be attached to it and the sense traditionally but erroneously attached to it by theologians. It is, that is to say, a non-paradoxical form of R-thesis that Feuerbach is advancing.

He does, nevertheless, insist on some continuity between what has been said in religion and his interpretation of it. For he claims to be doing no more than to make explicit what is already implicit in religion itself:

> I . . . let religion speak for itself; I constitute myself only as its listener and interpreter, not its prompter. Not to invent, but to discover, to "unveil existence", has been my sole object; to *see* correctly my whole endeavour. It is not I, but religion that worships man, although religion, or rather theology, denies this; it is not I, an insignificant individual, but religion that denies the God who is *not* man, but only an *ens rationis*—since it makes God become man, and then constitutes this God, not distinguished from man, having a human form, human feelings, and human thoughts, the object of its worship and veneration. I have only found the key to the cipher of the Christian religion, only extricated its true meaning from the web of contradictions and delusions called theology . . . religion itself, not indeed on the surface, but fundamentally, not in intention or according to its own suppositions, but in its heart, in its essence, believes in nothing else than the truth and divinity of human nature (EC xxxvi).

Feuerbach, then, wishes to show religion as man's relation

to his own true nature. He tries to do this by means of what he calls "empirical" or "historico-philosophical" analysis. It is an "empirical" analysis in so far as he claims to be looking for the meaning of religion in human experience. It is "historical" in that it is supported by citations of theological writings designed to show how theology itself pointed in the direction of "anthropology". Had this been evidence to the effect that the reasoning provided by theologians for their conclusions pointed to *different* ("anthropological") conclusions, he might have made out a strong case for saying that theology is only an oblique way of talking about human nature. But his citations seem only to support a Feuerbachian conclusion if they themselves are interpreted in a Feuerbachian way. They tend, that is to say, to presume, rather than lend independent support to, his analysis of religious doctrines.

How this is so may be brought out by a typical example of such "evidence". Feuerbach claims that "the idea of the future life is . . . nothing else than the idea of true, perfected religion, freed from the limits and obstructions of this life" (EC 190 fn.). Two quotations are adduced in support of this claim. Firstly, he quotes St Bernard—"*Dum sumus in hoc corpore, peregrinamur ab eo qui summe est*"; then, from Luther— "As long as we live, we are in the midst of death". Now, considered as independent evidence, these citations do not lend support to Feuerbach's "nothing else" interpretation. As such, the most they can be considered to support is the quite orthodox claim that the future life has, as *one* of its characteristics, this feature of being freed from "the limits and obstructions of this life". It seems, if anything, that such citations can only *bear out* the general interpretation offered by Feuerbach. They do not seem to give independent support to it.

We may turn, therefore, to the general interpretation. Feuerbach rejects the traditional understanding of religious claims as being about a transcendent being on the ground that, so construed, they give rise to inescapable contradictions. His account of the development of religion is "dialectical" in character. It is given, that is to say, in terms of thesis, antithesis and synthesis. The first stage is that of man's alienation from himself, from his own essential nature. This alienation gives rise to[1] a second stage, in which man projects or objectifies this nature, such that it is seen as another being, standing over against mankind. But,

> ... when this projected image of human nature is made an object of reflection, of theology, it becomes an inexhaustible mine of falsehoods, illusions, contradictions, and sophisms (EC. 214).

Hence a third stage may be anticipated in which men will recognize these absurdities for what they are and thus become reconciled to themselves once more. This is the stage of self-consciousness in religion, of which Feuerbach claimed to be the herald. It is, he thought, part of the "historical progress" of religion that "what was formerly contemplated and worshipped as God is now perceived to be something *human*" (EC 13).

An example of Feuerbach's procedure is to be found in his demonstration of a "contradiction" in the idea of 'the existence of God'. (Ch. XX) He says that theologians must claim an *empirical* existence for God, yet all the proofs point to no more than a *conceptual* existence. Hence God's existence is both sensational and non-sensational, according to the theologians, which is impossible. So runs Feuerbach's argument. But then the contradiction he imputes to the theologians depends on assumptions which they would be reckless to share. It would be a rash theologian who conceded that one cannot intelligibly speak of a *real* existence unless one speaks of an *empirical* existence. For once such a concession is made, the argument quickly moves to an anti-theological conclusion:

> The existence of God must therefore be in space—in general, a qualitative, sensational existence. But God is not seen, not heard, not perceived by the senses. He does not exist for me, if I do not exist for him; if I do not believe in a God, there is no God for me.

[1] It is not clear whether Feuerbach thought of this alienation as *preceding* the rise of religion or as being *constituted* by it. For he gives no indication of what, apart from religion, brings about man's estrangement from his true nature.

If I am not devoutly disposed, if I do not raise myself above the life of the senses, he has no place in my consciousness. *Thus he exists only in so far as he is felt, thought, believed in*;—the addition "for me" is unnecessary. His existence therefore is a real one, yet at the same time not a real one;—a spiritual existence, says the theologian (EC 200, italics mine).

This argument is characteristic of those employed by Feuerbach to show contradictions in theological doctrines. It starts with certain presuppositions as to what will count as something ("real existence"), goes on to show how the doctrine in question cannot consistently be construed in the way intended, and concludes by suggesting an "anthropological" construction for it. Thus Feuerbach, eager as ever to allow that theologians do mean *something* by what they say, even vouchsafes what might be meant by speaking of God as "existing". And, in droll fashion, he concludes by making his account appear to square with the theologian's talk of "spiritual existence". Only, for him, "spiritual existence" means "existence only in the mind".

5. FEUERBACH'S EPISTEMOLOGICAL ASSUMPTIONS

At the heart of Feuerbach's critique of theology lie certain epistemological tenets concerning what can be intelligibly said about how things are. These are not always argued for explicitly, but two such tenets are offered some support. These are: (1) that no being can conceive of any higher nature than its own; and (2) that for us to have a concept of finitude, there must actually be something *in*finite of which we are conscious. In subscribing to (1) it is clear that he is committed to rejecting the intelligibility of talk about God. His acceptance of (2) reveals an area of common ground which he shares with a number of religious thinkers in so far as it involves him in a form of Cosmological Argument with a difference. The difference is, of course, that it is an argument for the existence of what replaces God in his anthropology, namely, what he calls "the Species".

If these two tenets are examined, the outline of Feuerbach's

position becomes clearer. They are indeed connected right at
the beginning of his book. For, on the view there put forward,
man is said to differ from "the brutes" both in having religions
and in being, in the strict sense, conscious. "Consciousness
in the strict sense is present only in a being to whom his species,
his essential nature, is an object of thought" (EC 1). But if both
having religion and being conscious of his essential nature
are identical with man's essential characteristic, they must—
so the argument runs—be the same characteristic differently
expressed. Thus the object of religion is man's essential nature.

It is likely that Feuerbach has here fallen into a trap set for
himself by relying on such notions as 'essence' and 'essential'.
For he gives no reason for supposing—what his argument
seems to suppose—that there is but one essential feature of man,
hence that these different descriptions *must* be of the same
feature. Certainly there is a premiss missing from his argument,
which is needed to license the conclusion that religion "is and
can be nothing else but the consciousness which man has of his
own—not finite and limited, but infinite nature" (EC 2).
And this premiss would need to affirm the identity of all man's
essential features.

Feuerbach does not, however, rest his case on so slight and
doubtful a piece of reasoning as this. He goes on to argue that
"a really finite being has not even the faintest adumbration,
still less consciousness, of an infinite being, for the limit of the
nature is also the limit of the consciousness" (EC 2). By the
same token, a really finite creature would have no consciousness of its finitude. Thus the human individual, who is aware
of his own finitude, must be aware of something by contrast
with which he is able to recognize himself as merely finite.
That "something" would itself need to be infinite. But man
cannot conceive of anything higher than his own nature.
Hence there must be some sense in which man's nature is
itself infinite. But this is patently untrue of our *individual*
natures. Therefore our true nature must lie outside ourselves
as individuals in the species. It is the species itself which is
infinite.

Some light is thrown on Feuerbach's position at this point
by his treatment of the doctrine of the Trinity. This doctrine
is, he recognizes, incompatible with a view of the deity as a
self-contained individual uninfluenced by all others. For he
argues:

> ... from a solitary God the essential need of duality, of love, of
> community, of the real, completed self-consciousness, of the *alter
> ego*, is excluded. This want is therefore satisfied by religion thus:
> in the still solitude of the Divine Being is placed another, a second,
> different from God as to personality, but identical with him in
> essence. . . . Participated life is alone true, self-satisfying, divine
> life:—this simple thought, this truth, natural, immanent in man,
> is the secret, the supernatural mystery of the Trinity. But religion
> expresses this truth, as it does every other, in an indirect manner,
> i.e. inversely, for it here makes a general truth into a particular
> one, the true object into a predicate, when it says: God is parti-
> cipated life, a life of love and friendship (EC 67).

Man's true nature, according to Feuerbach, does not lie in
himself as an individual but in his relation to other men. But
more than this, each man is to his fellow a "representative of
the species" (EC 158). There is, that is to say, a "universal
significance" in the relations between individuals, for not only
does each represent the *alter ego*, the "objective conscience" of
the other, but each is the "mediator" (EC 159) between the
other and the "sacred idea of the species". But more than this
still, humanity is not—contrary to what some of his critics[2]
have supposed—a mere "abstraction" (EC 153). It is, for
Feuerbach, something actual. Nor does it have to be understood as some kind of "concrete universal". The thesis is that
the divine attributes form the *essence* of the species, but "it has
its complete *existence* only in all men taken together" (EC 152).

The thought seems to be that the essence of a man's humanity
is brought home to him by other men. In this way he becomes
aware of an ideal of humanity by contrast with which he

[2] This was one objection made by Marx in his *Eleven Theses on Feuerbach*.
Karl Barth also speaks of Feuerbach's "fictitious concept of generalized
man" in his *From Rousseau to Ritschl*, London (SCM Press) and New York
(Harper & Row) 1959, p. 361.

sees himself as limited *qua* individual. In religion this ideal is made into a super-human individual who judges the inadequacies of individual men. The Incarnation doctrine, according to Feuerbach, is at once the representation of the humanity of God and the divinity of human nature. Only Christianity mistakenly understands this doctrine as God becoming a man to make men like him. Feuerbach holds it to be God showing himself to be man. In support of this he quotes St Augustine's dictum *"Deus homo factus est, ut homo Deus fieret"*.

There are passages, it should be said, which would lend some support to the view that Feuerbach treats the species as *idealized* human nature. This is particularly so in passages where he seems to suggest that religion as traditionally practised consists in objectivizing a human ideal and worshipping it as something superhuman. He seems almost to say as much in the following passage:

> The yearning of man after something above himself is nothing else than the longing after the perfect type of his nature, the yearning to be free from himself, *i.e.*, from the limits and defects of his individuality (EC 281).

But even here there is no reason for supposing that he is speaking of what he elsewhere calls "an object of mere thought" rather than the actual human race. He makes his position unambiguous when he says that

> *only men taken together are what man should and can be.* All men are sinners. Granted: but they are not all sinners in the same way; on the contrary, there exists a great and essential difference between them. One man is inclined to falsehood, another is not. . . . Thus, in the moral as well as in the physical and intellectual elements, men compensate for each other, so that, *taken as a whole, they are as they should be, they present the perfect man* (EC 155f., my italics).

Feuerbach's view is that the human race is itself, taken as a whole, perfect. And indeed, on his thesis, this is necessarily so. It would make no sense for a man to deny it, since a man cannot conceive of anything higher than his own species. He can, of course, think of himself as finite and imperfect, but not so the human race. As Feuerbach puts it:

... it is a ludicrous and even culpable error to define as finite and limited what constitutes the essence of man, the nature of the species, which is the absolute nature of the individual. Every being is sufficient to itself. No being can deny itself, *i.e.* its own nature; no being is a limited one to itself. Rather every being is in and by itself infinite—has its God, its highest conceivable being, in itself. Every limit of a being is cognizable only by another being out of and above him (EC 7).

These epistemological assumptions are crucial to Feuerbach's reduction of theology to "anthropology". In particular, it must, from his point of view, be unintelligible to claim that the human race as such is finite or imperfect. Yet it might be objected that such a claim is perfectly intelligible. For example, there is no difficulty in thinking of the human race as finite in total duration of existence or as finite in collective power or knowledge. On the face of it, Feuerbach is making use of standards of intelligibility which are somewhat arbitrary.

One consideration which Feuerbach produces in favour of this tenet is that a bad poet who recognizes his poetry for what it is worth is less limited in his nature than one who is contented with what he writes (EC 8). Since one's understanding stretches no further than one's nature, one cannot intelligibly suppose that nature to be limited. But this is not borne out by the case of the bad poets. For it is only one of the poets whose lack of excellence as a poet is thus linked to inability to appreciate the worth of what he writes. In that case the nature and the understanding do, so to speak, keep a-pace. But the poet who recognizes the poor quality of his own writing does not *eo ipso* become a better poet. Here the understanding does, if one may so speak, run ahead of the nature.

There is, in any case, no difficulty in our arriving at a notion of infinity simply by being able to grade things into a series in some respect. Suppose, for example, it is thought that divinity is manifested by the absence of feeling. One person can thus be seen to have less feeling than another, and a being can be conceived as having no feeling whatsoever, as infinitely dispassionate. An infinite being could thus be conceived of whose nature was higher than human nature in this respect, without its having to exist to make possible our having such a notion of it. Neither of Feuerbach's chief epistemological tenets can be insisted upon.

Thus presented, Feuerbach's manner of accounting for religion does not seem plausible. For it is difficult to find such standards of intelligibility acceptable which set the limits of understanding at the limits of human nature. They seem arbitrary in the sense that they do not express adequately the features of religious claims by virtue of which people do find them unintelligible. Feuerbach does not establish the connection between human nature and the understanding in a way which can give rise to quite general standards of intelligibility.

6. EPISTEMOLOGY AND HUMAN NATURE

Philosophers have not uncommonly tried, as Feuerbach did, to derive such general standards of what it makes sense to say from considerations about human nature. In some cases, however, this has—at least in practice—been a somewhat subsidiary feature of their argument. Hume, for example, entitled his major philosophical work *A Treatise of Human Nature*. His avowed intention was to put "the science of human nature" on a secure footing by bringing "experimental philosophy" to the study of "moral subjects". This aim is to be found also in his *Enquiry*. Here he declares that he is going to examine human nature, appealing only to "experience" and "observation" in order

> to find those principles, which regulate our understanding, excite our sentiments, and make us approve or blame any particular object, action, or behaviour (EHU 5f.).

At first sight, he admits, it may look as if nothing is "more unbounded than the thought of man" (EHU 18). But what we find, upon a closer examination of the matter, is that

> it is really confined within very narrow limits, and that all this creative power of the mind amounts to no more than the faculty of compounding, transposing, augmenting, or diminishing the materials afforded by the senses and experience (EHU 19).

In practice, the thesis about the limits of human thought is subordinated to a thesis about the conditions under which words can come to have meaning. (See above, Section 2) Criticism of Hume has, accordingly, been most commonly directed against this latter thesis. But it is noteworthy that Hume himself, in speaking of the frailty of our faculties, seems almost to regard epistemology as a branch of "the science of human nature".

However that may be, Hume certainly thought that it was possible to reach conclusions about the limits of human understanding through a study of human nature. When one looks at the conclusions to which he comes, they turn out to bear a striking resemblance to the terms in which he sets up his inquiry in the first place. For he resolves to confine himself, in the name of science, to what can be observed of human nature. (THN xx) And just this stricture is reflected in his conclusions about the limits of human understanding. For it turns out that all our ideas are derived from our senses.

Nor should such a consequence be surprising. For restrictions of one kind or another must be placed on the conduct of any inquiry which pretends to be at all rigorous. These will be restrictions, for example, on what considerations will be admitted as relevant to the inquiry. If the inquiry is to be into the limits of human understanding, then some epistemological restrictions on the inquiry itself are inevitable. But then only inconsistency could prevent these initial restrictions being reflected in its conclusions. Hume's position may thus be likened to that of a fisherman who, having always used a particular size of mesh in his nets, concludes that there are no fish smaller than that size. To suppose that there could be an epistemologically neutral inquiry into human nature for the purpose of making epistemological discoveries is mistaken. Such a programme can only beg the question at the outset. In this sense no basis can be found in human nature for theses about what it makes sense to say.

In just this way Feuerbach begs the question against his theological opponents. His "anthropology" is also intended as a science of human nature. He claims indeed that he is "nothing but *a natural philosopher in the domain of mind*" (EC xxiv). He does, equally, not distinguish epistemology from the study of human nature. His thesis that no creature can conceive of a higher nature than its own, hence that the highest nature it can conceive *is* its own, relies on his ill-developed view that the measure of the nature is also the measure of the understanding (EC 8). His "science" of human nature is, therefore, not so much an empirical investigation as a working out of theses of a non-empirical character.

Kant's account in his *Critique of Pure Reason* takes him some way towards the view that epistemology is itself a kind of study of human nature, i.e. of human cognitive faculties. This is due in no small measure to his recognition that his thesis about the sensible character of human awareness of the world *is* a thesis about human nature. When he says that "our intuition is sensible", this should be understood with some stress on the word "our". And this has considerable significance for the way in which he restricts the use of the pure concepts of the under-standing. For, he notes, these concepts as such extend to "objects of intuition in general" (CPR, B 148f.). Were human intuition of a non-sensory kind, we should indeed be quite able to apply these concepts intelligibly outside sense-experience. But since experience is our only mode of awareness of anything outside ourselves, these concepts must be restricted in their range of intelligible application to what can be encountered in experience. Without such a restriction, these concepts (see above, Section 3) would lack "body and meaning" so far as we are concerned. But, while this limitation is valid for all human beings (CPR, A 27/B 43), *we* are in no position to say what holds for other thinking beings (CPR, B 72).

It should be noted that the view of religion as being a matter of human experience is ruled out at the beginning of Kant's First Critique. It is true that he holds belief in God to have some instrumental value for scientific inquiry and indeed to be required by ethics. But his thesis about human nature makes human relations with God at best indirect. It is, indeed, difficult to see at what point someone who wished to find room for religious experience could best take his departure from Kant's position, if not from his premissed thesis about human nature. He would be prevented from doing this only by such plausibility as attaches to the "critical philosophy" as a whole. For Kant does not argue for his thesis that human intuition is sensible at all.

To sum up: theses about human nature cannot be thought to provide a *basis* for setting up as universally valid any standards for what it makes sense to say. For such standards must already have been pre-supposed in any account of human nature which could appear to provide such a basis. There is not, in other words, the desired independence of suitable accounts of human nature from epistemological considerations. Thus one man may wish to say that men are made in the image of God, stand in some relation to God and may have knowledge of him. Another may deny this, saying that God is made in the image of man (is a projected father-image, or whatever) and that such "knowledge" is wholly illusory. The issue between them cannot be *decided* by appealing to an account of human nature. For any account of human nature which would provide an answer one way or the other would beg the question against the opposing view.

III

LANGUAGE, EXPERIENCE AND REALITY

THERE ARE, it has been suggested, three main sources from which support has been drawn for holding U-theses or R-theses about religious assertions. In the previous chapter consideration has been given to attempts to found such theses on an account of human nature. It has been argued that such attempts cannot succeed. There remain therefore two other possible sources which might provide support for such theses. These will now be considered in turn.

7. LANGUAGE AND REALITY

Some philosophers[1] have tried to argue that what gives sense to what we say is a possible correspondence between the language we use, on the one hand, and states of affairs, on the other. On such a view, reality consists of states of affairs which obtain quite independently of any language in which we might try to describe them. Our simple descriptions of the world will be true if, and only if, they correspond to actual states of affairs. They will be false given only a lack of correspondence between them and any state of affairs. Other more complex assertions are to be analyzed in such a way that they may be seen to be equivalent to a set of such simple descriptions. Any putative statement about the world which is found to be neither a simple description nor equivalent to a set of such

---

[1] A view rather like this seems to have been held by the early Wittgenstein in his *Tractatus Logico-Philosophicus* (1922), new translation by D. F. Pears and B. F. McGuinness, London (Routledge & Kegan Paul) and New York (Humanities Press) 1961, but his position is too complex to admit of summary exposition here.

descriptions cannot be thought to state anything. It is, in other words, not a genuine statement at all, since no sense can be attached to the claim which it attempts to make.

Despite the many facets and complications which attach to particular formulations of this view, there is a persuasion underlying it which may be expressed quite simply. It is, that language, in so far as it may be used to make intelligible claims about the world, can be shown to conform, directly or indirectly, to a particular paradigm. The paradigm is provided by certain simple descriptions,[2] e.g. "There is a pipe in my pocket" or "That is red". For such simple descriptions of what is the case seem to stand in a direct, uncomplicated relation to reality.

There is little doubt that it is *in some sense* quite true that such descriptions do stand in a direct, uncomplicated relation to reality. The question is, whether the sense in which it is true is the sense which this account of language seems to require. It is one which may be answered by considering a sceptical position which may appear to be allowed by the consideration that experience is required in order to know that this direct, uncomplicated relation obtains.

The sceptic may urge that too much is claimed by those who have spoken as if there were such a *direct* relation between language and reality. Surely, he may object, the *most* that could be said is that such claims stand in a direct relation to *observable* reality? He may even wish to insist that what is called "observable reality" is no more than *mere appearance*, or at any rate that we could never know that it *is* more than this. Over against a more radically sceptical position as this, we may be inclined to sympathize with a staunch insistence on a tight connection between how things are observed to be and how they actually are. But care must be taken in the way this connection is expressed.

---

[2] It does not matter, for present purposes, what best exemplifies a simple description. It would, however, be of some importance in developing such a view of language with the purpose of ruling out certain discourse as unintelligible.

It will not do, for instance, to content ourselves with the bland assertion that it must be obvious that how things are "in reality" does *correspond* to how they are observed to be. For it is not possible to identify separately the items of such a supposed correspondence in this kind of case. We are not, that is to say, in a position to check whether or not the correspondence holds. To do this we should have to be able to line up things as they are "in reality" on one side and things as we observe them to be on the other. If, *per impossibile*, we could do this, we should then be in a position to compare the two to see if they tally. But the basis for such a comparison does not exist.

That this is so may be brought out by contrasting this kind of case with the kind of case on which it is mis-modelled. Suppose we wish to find out whether two pieces of fabric "match" each other. All we need to do is to place them together and look to see whether their colours correspond. We can do this because the two pieces of fabric are separately identifiable if only through occupying different spatial positions. It is just this condition which is not satisfied by the distinction between how things are observed to be and how they really are. For we have no dealings with things as they really are *unless* they are dealings we have *in* our dealings with what we encounter through observation. Some philosophers, notoriously Kant, have expressed this point by saying that we have only to do with "appearances". But to say this is to accept the correspondence model, albeit sceptically. What we should do, rather, is to reject the correspondence model altogether.

It is tempting to counter the sceptic's argument by saying that there must be this connection because that is what is meant by "observation" or, more strictly, "observation *under normal conditions*". What we *mean*, for example, when we say that something is observed "under normal conditions" to be red is, simply, that it *is* red. Anyone who supposes to the contrary must either have misunderstood the language of observation or be choosing to use terms in a curious way.

The sceptic may, however, wish to resist this way of construing the issue. For it puts the assertion "If anything is observed under normal conditions to be red, it is red" on the same footing as "If anything is a bachelor, it is male". What necessity may attach to the former proposition does not seem to be the same as that attaching to the latter.[3] For whereas the latter assertion seems to depend for its necessity on certain conventions which govern our use of the words "bachelor" and "male", the former assertion seems to be necessary in a stronger sense.

But it has, in fact, been a matter of dispute amongst philosophers whether it is a *necessary* or a *contingent* matter that if anything is observed under normal conditions to be red, it really is red. Descartes, though he does not concern himself with this claim explicitly, seems to have been committed to regarding it as a *contingent* matter, one which might have been other than true, if true. For he introduces a sceptical device[4] in which an evil genius is postulated whose energies are devoted to deceiving him quite systematically. He does not claim that there is such a creature, only that the supposition that there is needs to be disproved. Unless it is disproved, the possibility will remain that he is quite deceived in supposing himself to have a body or in having experience of a world which is independent of himself. In such a quasi-dream world nothing will actually be as it seems to be. Nor is there anything *in experience itself* which can assure him that this is not so. That is why his scepticism is philosophical in character. To suppose that experience itself bears the stamp of being genuine (whatever that might mean) would be to beg the very question his sceptical device is designed to raise.

So it might be *contingently false* rather than *necessarily true* that what is observed to be red under normal conditions really is so. This would be the conclusion which Descartes' argument would

---

[3] I am indebted at this point to an argument by D. W. Hamlyn in his Inaugural Lecture at Birkbeck College (1965) entitled "Seeing things as they are". He is arguing in part against a view he expressed in his *The Psychology of Perception*, London (Routledge and Kegan Paul) and has included part of this argument in an appendix to a reprint of this book, shortly to be issued.

[4] cf. Meditation I of his *Meditations on the First Philosophy*.

have suggested had he not disposed of the evil genius hypothesis. It is disposed of on an *a priori* basis, by an argument which establishes, as Descartes thought, the existence of an omnipotent God of a non-deceiving character. His final conclusion commits him to a position from which our problematic proposition would be viewed as true. It is not altogether clear whether, on a Cartesian view, it would then be contingently or necessarily true. This depends on whether it is a contingent or a necessary matter that God is not a deceiver. And here difficulties arise on either side. If God can exercise choice in whether or not to deceive, which seems necessary for him to be the kind of being whose actions would be worthy of praise, then it is a contingent matter. On this view, the connection between appearance and reality does in general hold by the grace of God. But then, if it is a contingent matter, it might seem that less certainty attaches to the rejection of the evil genius hypothesis than Descartes needs.

That such a radically different account of the status of this claim appears to be possible should make us pause before treating it in the same way as "bachelors are male". For saying that it is a matter of how we use words does not help to understand what is wrong about the position Descartes is committed to. Saying this merely obscures what needs to be distinguished. But in what does the necessity of the claim that whatever is observed under normal conditions to be red really is red consist? How should it appear possible to deny it? Just what, indeed, is wrong with denying it? Some answer to these questions may be provided by looking more closely at the way in which Descartes arrives at his conclusion that our senses might always deceive us.

Descartes' starting-point is that "it is sometimes proved to me that these senses are deceptive".[5] He thinks that, if it is *sometimes* shown that the senses are mistaken, it needs to be shown that it is not *always* the case that they are mistaken. And this, at first sight, might seem reasonable enough. If the

---

[5] *Meditation* I. Quoted from *Philosophical Works of Descartes*, Vol. I (Tr. Haldane and Ross) Dover Edition, p. 145.

buses on a given route are sometimes late, we might well wonder whether they were not always late. Moreover, and this is the point at issue, it would at least *make sense* to suppose that they might always be late. But the bus analogy is deceptive. For whereas we can find out that the buses were always late by just the means that we would find out that they are sometimes late, we could not hope to find out that our senses *always* deceived us by the means which we use to find out that they do *sometimes* deceive us. For to do that we should have to *rely* on our senses. And we would involve ourselves in self-contradiction if we suppose that we could, while relying on the evidence of our senses, discover them to be wholly unreliable.

One way of putting this point is to say that our means of telling whether or not our senses are deceiving us on a particular occasion are swallowed up by the Cartesian doubt. They themselves, that is to say, are being called into question. And it is just in this respect that the bus analogy breaks down. For our means of telling whether or not the buses on a given route are late or not remain unaffected by our considering whether this is always rather than merely sometimes the case. But this is not so for sense-deception. For to suppose that our senses might deceive us *always* is to abandon the means of distinguishing veridical and illusory experience to which we appeal in telling that they do *sometimes* deceive us.

It is not difficult now to see where Descartes' reasoning has gone wrong. For, in order to launch his argument, he makes use of the premiss that "it is sometimes proved" that our senses are deceptive. In doing so he tacitly endorses the means normally available to us for distinguishing illusions, hallucinations, and so on, from veridical perception. But this premiss is not available to him if he is going to hypothesize that our senses might *always* deceive us. Only by rejecting such a premiss could he consistently entertain such a hypothesis. But this places him in a dilemma. For either he accepts these means or he does not. If he does, he cannot consistently introduce his sceptical device of an evil genius. If he does not, it is not clear how this premiss could otherwise be established and hence how such a line of sceptical argument could even begin. Descartes seems to be impaled on the first horn of this dilemma. His argument makes it seem possible to deny a necessary connection between how things are observed to be under normal conditions and how they actually are. But we will only be seduced by this apparent possibility if we accept a misleading analogy.

In *almost* every case, it does follow from its *sometimes* being true that p (where "p" stands for *any* proposition whatever) that it would *make sense* (even if it would be false) to claim that it is *always* true that p. This rule will hold if we substitute "the buses on route 9A are late" for p. But it does not hold universally. It does not, in particular, hold if we substitute "the evidence of our senses is mistaken" for p. It does not hold in this case because there are some substitution instances of p, of which this is one, where knowing what it would be like for p sometimes to be true does not bring with it knowledge of what it would be like for p to be always true.

The necessity which attaches to those exceptions which disprove the rule on which the Cartesian argument relies consists, it seems, in the fact that it would make no sense to deny them. Descartes' evil genius hypothesis may appear to confer some degree of intelligibility upon the hypothesis of universal sense-deception. But in fact it merely echoes and does not give sense to such an idea. To give sense to such an idea, one would need to find an alternative basis which is not itself founded on the language of experience. It is because Descartes' evil genius hypothesis itself depends upon the premiss that our senses do sometimes deceive us that it is infected by the same lack of intelligibility as has been shown to undermine his hypothesis of universal sense-deception. It cannot therefore do anything to explain what universal sense-deception would be like.

I shall return to this point in Section 9. What we have been considering here is the status of claims which connect how things are observed to be under normal conditions and how they actually are. Suffice it to observe that if the necessity of such claims does consist in its making no sense to deny them, then a tight connection has been found of the kind desired to oppose scepticism. This has been done without relying on that form of U-thesis which attempts to construe reality as that which gives language sense. In particular we may avoid in this way making use of the unworkable model of correspondence.

8. MEANING AND VERIFIABILITY

It has been mentioned that Kant based his epistemological theses upon considerations about human nature, in particular on the claim that human "intuition" is sensible. Ayer's presentation of his form of positivism is in some respects set up in contrast with that of Kant. For example, he takes Kant to task for making "the impossibility of a transcendent metaphysics . . . a matter of fact" (LTL 34) because it depends upon such considerations. Ayer's criterion of verifiability is intended, by contrast, to make the impossibility of such a metaphysic a "matter of logic". Hence he accepts the label "logical positivist" as applying to his position.

One way he expresses[6] his criterion for deciding "the genuineness of apparent statements of fact" is as follows:

> We may say that a sentence is factually significant to any given person if, and only if, he knows how to verify the proposition which it purports to express—that is, if he knows what observations would lead him, under certain conditions, to accept the proposition as being true, or reject it as being false. If, on the other hand, the putative proposition is of such a character that the assumption of its truth, or falsehood, is consistent with any assumption whatsoever concerning the nature of his future experience, then, as far as he is concerned, it is, if not a tautology, a mere pseudoproposition. The sentence expressing it may be emotionally significant to him; but it is not literally significant (LTL 35).

[6] I have confined myself to less formal expressions of this criterion and to more general criticisms of them as I wish my treatment to bear on other expressions of this form of U-thesis. For more rigorous treatment of Ayer's formulations, see, for example, C. G. Hempel's article in *Revue Internationale de Philosophie* (1950) on the empiricist criterion of meaning. It is reprinted in *Logical Positivism* (ed. Ayer and R. Winch), Illinois (Free Press of Glencoe) 1959.

In his Introduction to the Second Edition of *Language, Truth and Logic*, Ayer suggests that his verification principle should be regarded as a non-arbitrary definition (LTL 16). He suggests it should be regarded as a *definition*, since it does not—as his critics had not been slow to point out—meet the requirement of being itself verifiable. It could not therefore satisfy the standard of factual significance which it articulates. It is, however, a *non-arbitrary* definition, since it accords—or so Ayer maintains—with the way in which scientific hypotheses and "common-sense statements" are in practice "habitually understood". It is put forward, that is to say, as an account of the features by which we do in such matters make sense of some claims and fail to make sense of others. It is persuasive in character only in so far as the same hard-headed approach is commended towards all putative claims of fact whatsoever. The suggestion seems to be that this criterion works so satisfactorily for those claims whose standards of intelligibility it purports to describe that it is reasonable to take it as universally binding on all putatively factual claims whatever. To the extent that this is a *non-sequitur*, the definition must be seen as *persuasive* rather than *descriptive* in relation, for example, to the claims of religion.

Ayer attaches considerable importance to the distinction between "practical verifiability" and "verifiability in principle". Any claim which can in practice be verified will be for that reason verifiable "in principle". But *not vice-versa*. Ayer gives the following example of a proposition which is "conceivably but not actually verifiable":

> A simple and familiar example of such a proposition is the proposition that there are mountains on the farther side of the moon. No rocket has yet been invented which would enable me to go and look at the farther side of the moon, so that I am unable to decide the matter by actual observation. But I do know what observations would decide it for me, if, as is *theoretically conceivable*, I were once in a position to make them. And therefore I say that the proposition is verifiable *in principle*, if not in practice, and is accordingly significant (LTL 36, italics mine).

It will be remembered that we saw earlier how philosophers

tended to introduce the contrast between what was "in principle" possible and what was possible "in practice" as a distinction between what it *made sense* to suppose possible and what is, *as a matter of fact*, possible. And it seems that some such contrast is intended by Ayer. For he wishes to make such remarks as that "one cannot conceive of an observation which would enable one to determine whether the Absolute did, or did not, enter into evolution and progress" (LTL 36). But if he does intend to use "conceivably" verifiable as a synonym for verifiable "in principle", the question arises as to what standards are involved here. When he speaks, that is, of something as "theoretically conceivable", to what *theory* is Ayer appealing? A criterion is needed which guides the use of Ayer's criterion, a criterion which will enable us to tell whether or not something is verifiable *in principle*. Otherwise the verifiability criterion will be ineffective against contested cases.

Ayer, surprisingly, does not seem to have recognized this. He gives himself something of a walk-over by confining his attention to examples which are either all but verifiable or are admitted on all sides to be such that experience would not be relevant to deciding them. His example of the mountains on the farther side of the moon will readily be seen as too easy, since verifiability in practice is now possible with regard to it. His example of a putative claim which is not verifiable in principle does nothing to bring out the unintelligibility he claims against it, as is true also of his treatment of the claim that "the world of sense-experience was altogether unreal" (LTL 39). Nor is it surprising that he should fail to do this. For his use of phrases like "in principle" leaves his account vague at just the point where sharpness is critical.

It has thus been possible for some philosophers of religion to insist, within the letter but not the spirit of Ayer's criterion, that religious claims are in principle verifiable and, accordingly, factually significant. Hick, for example, argues that the possibility of certain experiences which would assure us of the reality of God ensures "the factual, true-or-false character of the claim that God . . . exists" (FK 199).

These are, *first*, an experience of the fulfilment of God's purpose for ourselves, as this has been disclosed in the Christian revelation, and *second*, in conjunction with the first, an experience of communion with God as he has revealed himself in the person of Christ (FK 187).

Now it is tempting to deny that it *is* possible in principle to have experiences of the kind which Hick describes. But Ayer, by using such unspecified phrases as "in principle", has provided a blank cheque which would seem to license such an "eschatological verification". This inadequacy of Ayer's criterion does, of course, cut both ways. If it is too vague to handle problematic cases, it may not rule out religious discourse. But equally it cannot be relied upon to guarantee the intelligibility of discourse which can be made to satisfy it. The factual significance or otherwise of religious discourse must be shown in some other way.[7]

I shall not discuss the merits of Ayer's "definition" as a *persuasive* one. For it has not been shown to be adequate as a *description* of the standards of intelligibility upon which scientists rely. It is questionable whether, even if it was adequate as an account of scientific standards of intelligibility, this would warrant claiming it to be adequate for all factual claims whatever. But, *unless* it is at least adequate as a description of scientific standards, it can provide no basis for a U-thesis. And just this adequacy seems jeopardized by not further specifying what is meant by "theoretically conceivable", "in principle" or "conceivable" in speaking of verification.

It seems natural enough to say that if we do wish to specify further what is meant by "theoretically conceivable" the theory to which we should turn is scientific theory. And this is what seems to be the practice even of physicists who have been much influenced by positivism. H. Dingle,[8] for example, has

---

[7] Hick himself seems to rely increasingly on other considerations. This is partly because, if I understand him correctly, he thinks it may be that verification is only available to the faithful (cf. FK 192f.). This seems to point to something like a B-thesis, Hick's version of which I shall discuss in Section 24 below.

[8] *Science and Human Experience*, London (Williams & Norgate) and New York (Macmillan) 1931.

advocated something like a positivist account of the Principle of Indeterminacy. It would be wrong, he stresses, to construe this principle as stating that, even though an electron does have a precise position and momentum, we cannot know both of them precisely at any given time. He writes:

> The principle of uncertainty does not limit the accuracy of our measurements; *it helps to define an electron.* The "uncertainty" of our determination is not a human failing; it is a measure of some property of the electron which can properly be defined only in terms other than those appropriate to sensible matter (op. cit., p. 64, italics mine).

Dingle, however, does *not* rule out the alternative thesis on the ground that no sense-experience could *in principle* enable one to decide both the position and momentum of an electron at any given time. On the contrary, although he does seem to rule out this alternative way of construing the principle as unintelligible, he does so on a basis which is incompatible with Ayer's:

> The rule of excluding inaccessibles from physics is often spoken of as if it were a fundamental philosophical principle; I think it is really only a rule of convenience. It supposes a kind of omniscience in us, by which *the physical world is necessarily composed only of that which, with our present knowledge and means of observation, we can conceivably detect* (op. cit., p. 66, italics mine).

On such an account, the present state of knowledge and currently available means of observation provide what basis there is for excluding hypotheses as unintelligible. To say this is to say that the standards of intelligibility involved in such exclusion are implicit in scientific theory itself. An immediate consequence of such an account is that the standards themselves do not hold good for all time any more than theories themselves do. It would be quite compatible with such an account for an hypothesis, at one time dismissed as unintelligible, to come to be regarded as true. I shall have something more to say on how this could be so in the following chapter. It is sufficient to note here that, if this is so, then there can be no universally valid standards of scientific intelligibility. Hence even if it were accepted—and Ayer gives no reason why it should be accepted

—that scientific standards would be the standards by which all putatively factual assertions are to be judged, these could not be given adequate expression in terms of a once-for-all criterion.

It might be thought that the force of these criticisms is directed only against Ayer's criterion as a sufficient condition for an assertion to be factually significant. It may be admitted that scientific theory may in practice have to do the work Ayer assigns to the notion of 'verifiability in principle'. But the criterion might still be put forward as a necessary condition. Indeed the rival interpretation ruled out by Dingle might be thought to be ruled out as satisfactorily by such a criterion. It should be said, however, that the vagueness of the "in principle" in the criterion makes even this use of it very intuitive.

These criticisms of Ayer's position would seem to bear against any attempt to set up general standards of scientific intelligibility and claim universal validity for them. For such attempts cannot but be caught between the vagueness of some "in principle" clause and the over-specific standards involved in science at any given time. One can only give them teeth by depriving them of any claim to universal validity. One can only give them a pretence of universal validity by depriving them of teeth.

9. SENSE AND "GRAMMAR"

The three main sources from which support has been sought for advancing quite general norms of intelligibility have now been examined. I have tried to argue on general lines that they do not and cannot provide the hoped-for support which would make U-theses or R-theses viable. It follows from these considerations that U-theses and R-theses are not tenable with regard to religious claims.

The argument, however, has not been purely negative. For the argument of Section 7 has, if sound, tended to support the view that the unintelligibility of the hypothesis of universal sense-deception is with respect to the language of observation. The argument of Section 8 has, if sound, tended to support a rather similar thesis. For it suggested that we should be speaking with reference to currently accepted scientific theory if we dismissed a hypothesis as "scientific nonsense". The suggestion would seem to be that the standards of what it makes sense to say are to be found *within* a given mode of discourse and do not stand *over against* it. This suggestion must now be considered at greater length.

Let us return to the problem posed by the Cartesian doubt whether it might not be the case that one's senses were deceiving one all the time. A difficulty was noted earlier in making sense of such a doubt. We can, it seems, attach sense to such doubts only where we have, as a background, accepted means of telling whether or not our senses are deceiving us. If we do provide this background, the Cartesian doubt is quite intelligible but patently unfounded. But if we remove the background, it is not clear just what the doubt is. The doubt must acquire a new background, a foothold outside the language of observation, if sense is to be given to it.

One might express Descartes' position as that of raising an "external question" about the language of observation itself. The question whether our senses sometimes deceive us is, by contrast, an "internal question",[9] one which is to be settled by the means provided within the language of observation. It is as an "internal question", that the possibility of universal sense-deception can be dismissed with a commonsensical negative. As an "external question" we do not know what to make of it. But how can such an external question be raised? Descartes himself does not succeed in showing us. For in assuming it to follow from that fact that our senses sometimes deceive us that it would at least make sense to suppose that they always do so, he breaks what might be termed a rule of "grammar" which is implicit in our language of observation.

[9] The terminology is that of R. Carnap, who uses it to make a largely similar distinction. See his article "Empiricism, Semantics and Ontology", *Revue Internationale de Philosophie* (1950).

In describing his mistake as one of "grammar", one would be distinguishing it from a mistake about a matter of fact. The use of the word "grammar" in this case may be justified by the similarity this kind of mistake has to that involved in such questions as "Where does the flame go when it goes out?" This use of the word "grammar" derives immediately from Wittgenstein's writings after 1930. He readily admitted its slightly unusual character. But we should be using his "jargon", he said at one point,[10] if we said that whether a sentence made sense or not depended on "whether it was constructed according to the rules of grammar". The distinction between sense and nonsense is reflected in the use which language has. We do not therefore need to consult a "book of grammar" to know how to talk sense.[11] Wittgenstein once said[12] that the word "God" was used in many grammatically different senses. In some religions it was so used that it would make sense to say that God had three arms. In others, however, it would not make sense to say that God had arms at all. Theology, according to Wittgenstein, could be thought of as "grammar". For grammar tells us "what kind of object anything is".[13] And theology tells us what it makes sense to say about God and what it does not make sense to say. When it is said,[14] for example, "You can't hear God speak to someone else, you can hear him only if you are being addressed", it is a *grammatical* and not a *matter-of-fact* remark which is being made. The sense in which it is "impossible" to overhear God speaking to someone is that it would make no sense to suppose that one could.

In describing theology as "grammar" Wittgenstein seems to be regarding it as concerned to articulate the standards of intelligibility implicit in the language of a given religion. It is not that there would not be such standards governing religious

[10] In his 1930–3 lectures at Cambridge, as reported by G. E. Moore in *Mind* 1954–5 and reprinted in Moore's *Philosophical Papers*, London (Allen & Unwin) 1959. See p. 276.

[11] *Zettel*, Oxford (Basil Blackwell) 1967, Sect. 297.

[12] *Philosophical Papers*, p. 312.

[13] *Philosophical Investigations*, Oxford (Basil Blackwell) 1953, I, Sect. 373.

[14] *Zettel*, Sect. 717.

discourse unless it was possible to appeal to theology. The point is rather that the standards which govern what it makes sense to say within a given field of discourse must be sought *within* that field of discourse itself. They cannot, that is to say, be imposed upon a field of discourse from the outside. The question "Can God be mocked?", for example, is a question about what it makes sense to say about God. It can only be considered within the context of a particular religion.

This line of reasoning would suggest that it does not make sense for a man to say: "I know this object has been observed under normal conditions to be red, but I doubt whether it really is so". Such a man would have failed to understand the grammar of talk about observation under normal conditions. And the penalty, if one may so speak, of breaking such a rule of grammar is that what is doubted, claimed or asked will not make sense. Descartes' hypothesis of universal sense-deception has to be treated as an "internal question" and hence as subject to the standards implicit in the language of observation. As such it is patently false. Yet as an "external question" it is unintelligible. It can only be judged by the standards implicit in the language of observation since no other standards are introduced by which it might be judged. Nor, in so far as our concept of observation under normal conditions is an adequate one, is there any ground for hoping that any other way could be found which would make such an hypothesis intelligible.

This is not to say that "external questions" can *never* be raised. Philosophy presents numerous examples. Berkeley (see Section 1 above) and Hume (see Section 2 above) did so in relation, respectively, to talk about "material substances" and "necessary connections between events". Unlike Descartes, they went at least some way towards providing themselves with an adequate footing for raising their questions. The conceptual changes they proposed were part and parcel with their attempts to refine a language of experience which could dispense with such talk.

What Descartes attempted to do, it might be said, was to

show that the language of observation needed the support of the language of religion. In attempting to do so he sought to establish that our conception of the world as independently real needs to be supported by a religious "conception of reality". For, on his argument, our senses may be trusted only because God may be trusted. But his difficulty—put in these metaphysical-sounding terms—is that he *begins* from the very "conception of reality" which he seeks to call in question. He cannot therefore be excused from criticism drawn from the terms appropriate to that conception of reality.

The point which should be emphasized here is that it is the *same* criticism which is being made of him, when it is said that Descartes is guilty of breaking a rule of *grammar* implicit in our language of observation, *or* that he presupposes the very *conception of reality* which he sets out to call in question. For his premiss that our senses are sometimes proved to have deceived us belongs, one might say, both to our language of observation *and* to the conception of reality *specified by* the grammar of that language. It makes sense to us as a claim which is subject to the criteria by which our use of perceptual terms is governed. As such, we know what it is for this premiss to be true. (We know indeed that, as a matter of fact, it *is* true.) But the claim that our senses might be deceiving us *all* the time, if it is to be other than patently false, must involve an attempt to break away from this language of observation. Yet it is only as subject to the standards of intelligibility implicit in this language that we can make sense of such a claim. It is not surprising, then, that we should find it unintelligible. This would not, however, rule out the possibility of our *coming* to make sense of such a claim. But we could only do so by embracing a conception of reality in terms of which, say, the evil genius hypothesis would make sense in its own right, without reliance on the problematic notion of universal deception. This possibility is a very far-fetched one in this case, but, as will be seen, it need not be so in all cases.

Given this account, we may express more sharply the view which is being commended over against the thesis that reality is what gives language sense. It may be said[15] that the distinction between what is to count as "real" and "unreal" is to be found in the language itself. The notion of 'correspondence with reality' cannot be used to give *content* to language, for *its* content needs to be specified by reference to the field of discourse into which it enters. Another way of putting this point is to say that talk about "reality" can only take place *within* some *conception* of reality. If we doubt whether what has been observed under conditions taken to be normal really is as it was observed to be, we can only have recourse to further observation. It is quite wrong to think of reality as standing over against conceptions of reality as "the objective criterion of their adequacy". For it is only *within* the context provided by a given conception of reality that talk of something's being real or unreal makes sense.

This seems to be the point made by Wittgenstein's remark: "Like everything metaphysical, the harmony between thought and reality is to be found in the grammar of the language" (*Zettel*, Section 55). This would suggest that grammatical propositions, in stating what it would not make sense to deny, articulate features of a conception of reality. Viewed from within the conception of reality in relation to which they enjoy their grammatical status, they appear as being in some way necessarily true. This is how it is with the claim "If anything is observed under normal conditions to be red, it really is red." Berkeley claimed, in effect, that the existence of God has just this status in relation to the language of experience. I shall consider, in Chapter IX, whether it could be said to have this status in relation to the language of religion.

In the meantime, however, further discussion is needed of the status of grammatical propositions. And this will form one topic of the next chapter.

[15] I owe this way of looking at the matter to Peter Winch. He makes a very similar point in his article "Understanding a primitive society", *American Philosophical Quarterly*, 1964, p. 309, reprinted in *Religion and Understanding* (ed. D. Z. Phillips), Oxford (Basil Blackwell) 1967, p. 13, which will be referred to hereinafter as "RU".

IV

INSIGHT AND UNDERSTANDING

IN THE previous chapter it was noted how "grammatical" remarks can indicate the limits of what it makes sense to say. The question must now be raised: What is the status of grammatical remarks themselves? In particular it must be asked: Can they correctly be described as "true" or "false"? An approach to these questions may be made by considering changes in "grammar" or, in other words, conceptual change.

10. THE NATURE OF CONCEPTUAL CHANGE

It is a commonplace observation that words may, in the course of time, come to change their meaning. When, for example, St Paul's Cathedral was built it was described by a contemporary writer as "aweful, artificial and contrived". Some knowledge of the history of the English language is involved in our recognizing that its architect and builders would have found such an account of their work wholly complimentary. These words have since changed their meaning, as words often do. The significance we attach to any such change depends on the point of view from which we regard it. Thus it is, for instance, a matter of regret to some people that the word "holiday" has largely lost its original meaning of "holy day", whereas it is no doubt a matter of satisfaction or indifference to others.

Where such changes in the meaning of words are sufficiently far-reaching, it may be appropriate to speak of *conceptual change*. The expression "far-reaching" is, of course, too vague to serve as a means of clarifying any distinction between conceptual change and changes which affect only the nuances of words. But such a clarification may be sought through a consideration of examples.

We no longer assume, in describing something as a "law of nature" or a "natural law", that it has been ordained by some higher being. And this seems to be a case where a change in our use of an expression reflects a conceptual change. For at one time people did believe that order in the course of events was to be attributed to the governing hand of a providence. Indeed, it is difficult to see how the word "law" could have been applied to the course of events at all, had this not been so.

This change may be seen by contrasting the views of Leibniz and Hume on laws of nature. Leibniz had argued that the law-like character of such so-called "laws" could never be derived from experience. "The senses can indeed help us after a fashion to know what is, but they cannot help us to know what *must* be or what cannot be otherwise."[1] For "although we have countless times tested the fact that every heavy body falls we are not sure that this is necessary until we have grasped the reason for it". It is only when we have grasped the reason why a good creator would have set up such a "subordinate regulation"[2] that we see the necessity in such a law. Thus "the final analysis of the laws of nature leads us to the most sublime principles of order and perfection, which indicate that the universe is the effect of a universal intelligent power".[3] Leibniz saw, as did Hume, that there could be no question of our observing any necessity of connection between events, however regularly conjoined they may be.

Unlike Leibniz, however, Hume thought we could have no idea of a law of nature which went beyond those regular conjunctions with which experience has provided us. The difference between a law of nature and a causal hypothesis lies, on such a view, in the fact that a law has been found to

---

[1] *Philosophical Papers and Letters* (tr. and ed. L. E. Loemker) Chicago University Press, 2 vols., p. 894.

[2] *Discourse on Metaphysics*, Section xvi.

[3] *Philosophical Papers and Letters*, p. 777f.

hold universally over a wide range of cases. In denying natural necessity, Hume was committed to a different concept of natural law, one which does not need to be understood in metaphysical or theological terms. In this, though not every respect, Hume might be credited with anticipating and perhaps even paving the way for a purely secular understanding of regularities in nature. For, as the expression "law of nature" is now used, it no longer makes sense to speak of laws of nature as being "broken" or "violated". What connection remains between laws of nature and, for example, laws of the land, is at best extremely tenuous. For though some philosophers of science have understood laws of nature as *rules*, they have not construed them as rules governing the events themselves. They have, rather, thought of them as rules which make possible inferences, and which are therefore useful for the purposes of measurement and prediction. It is true that scientists do still speak of phenomena *obeying* or not obeying laws. Non-crystalline substances, for example, are said not to obey Snell's law. But this is no more than a manner of speaking. The theological connotations of the expression "law of nature" or "natural law" have disappeared. And with their disappearance the concept has undergone a change.

One reason for speaking of *conceptual* change in such cases is that more may be involved than a change in the meaning of a particular word or expression. Indeed one may speak, as will shortly be brought out, of conceptual change even where no particular word or expression is retained. In such cases it is clearly a difficult matter to say with respect to what a change has taken place. But even in cases where a change has taken place in a given language, it need not be peculiar to that language. As with the expression "law of nature", the changes of meaning may be paralleled by changes in the meanings of words in other languages. It would seem strange here to deny that there is, in some sense, only one change involved in such a set of parallel changes. And this would be called a "conceptual change".

It may only be possible to express equivocally in respect of what a conceptual change has taken place. This seems to be the case with the concept 'law of nature'. For, if a suitable covering expression is sought which brings out what is common to the old and new concept, the nearest candidate would seem to be something like—"what accounts for regularity in the course of events". But if this way of putting it is saved from ambiguity, it is only through the vagueness of the expression "accounts for". Nor should this be a surprising feature. For the traditional understanding of what is involved in accounting for regularity in the course of events is by no means the same as that which now prevails. Whereas it was previously thought that such order had to be understood in terms of divine purpose[4] laws of nature are no longer thought of in this way, if indeed they are thought of as *explanations* of regularities at all.

A similar equivocation is involved in Hume's revision of the concept 'necessary connection':

> The necessary connection betwixt cause and effect is the foundation of our inference from one to another. The foundation of our inference is the transition arising from the accustomed union. They are, therefore, the same (THN 165).

Critics of Hume would, of course, be quick to point out the grotesque pun on the word "foundation" in this argument. For whereas the word "justification" might serve as a synonym for "foundation" in the first sentence, it cannot in the second. But, in defence of Hume, it might be replied that any covering phrase which would express the continuing element in a conceptual change would have to be ambiguous. The expression "foundation of our inference from cause to effect" is only one case. To complain of the pun is to complain of the proposed revision.

An important feature of conceptual change is that it is part of a changed understanding of the phenomena to which the concept in question is applied. It was formerly seen as a necessary matter that laws of nature were ordained by God. An observed regularity could not otherwise be held to be law-like.

---

[4] Leibniz, for example, thought that the rectilinear propagation of light was due to "God's decree to always carry out his plan by the easiest and most determined way" (*Discourse on Metaphysics*, Sect. xxi).

The change in the concept is, at least in part, a consequence of people ceasing to believe that order in the universe *has* to be understood in terms of divine purpose. Part of what is involved here is the recognition that theological considerations are not relevant to the conduct of scientific inquiry. This change might, therefore, be quite innocuously described as a "secularization" of the concept 'law of nature'.

There is a further aspect to conceptual change which may serve to distinguish it more sharply from less far-reaching changes in word usage. For a conceptual change involves a change in what it makes sense to say. The concept 'law of nature' can thus be seen to have changed in so far as it no longer makes sense to say, for example, that laws of nature can be "violated". We might equally speak here of a change in the "grammar" of our talk about laws of nature.

11. THE STATUS OF GRAMMATICAL REMARKS

Philosophers, following Kant, have commonly made use of a distinction between judgments which are "analytic" and those which are "synthetic" in character. An example of an "analytic" judgment is: "All bachelors are unmarried men". This type of claim tells us nothing about the world. In this case it tells us only about the concept 'bachelor'—it makes explicit what is implicit in that concept. Being an unmarried man adds nothing to the concept 'bachelor'. For it is already contained in the concept. An example of a "synthetic" judgment is: "All bachelors drive fast sports cars". This type of claim, by contrast, does tell us about the world. For it is in no way part of the concept 'bachelor' that we count as bachelors only people who drive fast sports cars. It is indeed a matter of fact whether or not it is true that bachelors do drive fast sports cars. Unlike "analytic" judgments, "synthetic" judgments can turn out to be false as a matter of fact.[5]

[5] Kant thought that there were some synthetic judgments which experience could not prove to be true or false. These he described as "synthetic *a priori*". Their truth could be established, he thought, quite independently of experience.

We can know, it has been said, that "analytic" judgments are true quite independently of experience. For we cannot fail to see their truth when we see that the predicate-concept (e.g. being an unmarried man) is contained in the subject-concept (e.g. bachelor). But we could only be entitled to speak in this way if we could justify speaking of any given concept as *the* concept of anything. There can, that is to say, only be analytic truths to the extent that it is an uncontentious matter what is included in a given concept. And to the extent that concepts do change it must be admitted that there is no uncontentious way of identifying them. There is, for example, no universal agreement as to how the concept 'law of nature' should be explicated. No one is entitled to speak of *his* concept 'law of nature' as *the* concept. It seems, therefore, that analytic truths can only be expressed regarding concepts which are not subject to dispute.

There are a number of different ways in which it might be possible to determine the identity of a concept in such a way that analytic truths may be made about it. One such way is provided by accounts of such truths which make their necessity depend wholly on human conventions. Ayer gives such an account in the following terms:

> . . . analytic propositions are necessary and certain . . . the reason why they cannot be confuted in experience is that they do not make any assertion about the empirical world. They simply record our determination to use words in a certain fashion. We cannot deny them without infringing the conventions which are presupposed by our very denial, and so falling into self-contradiction. And this is the sole ground of their necessity (LTL 84).

Ayer does not deny that conventions may change. It is, for him, "perfectly conceivable" that we might have employed different conventions from those which do in fact govern our use of words.

It seems clear that Ayer is not espousing a form of conventionalism which draws attention to the arbitrary character of the sounds and marks we make in speaking and writing. Such a form of conventionalism would be quite trivial. For example, we might employ the sign "3" to symbolize what we now symbolize by the sign "2", and *vice-versa*. In one sense we could be said thereby to have altered a convention such that it would be true to say "3 + 3 = 4" and "2 + 2 = 6". But the truth of the proposition expressed by "2 + 2 = 4" is quite unaffected by the conventions governing its mode of expression. These conventions do in any case equally bear upon the expression of synthetic as analytic propositions. And Ayer's conventionalism involves him in saying that there is a sense in which the truth of analytic propositions *but not* of all propositions whatever depends upon "linguistic conventions".

There are, however, two other forms of conventionalism which more closely resemble the view which Ayer appears to take. The weaker thesis barely merits being described as an "ism". It draws its rationale from the consideration that learning a language involves learning how to use words correctly. The standards of correctness and incorrectness are reflected in the established use which words have in the language. An established rule of language may equally, on such a view, be spoken of as a "linguistic convention". But no incontrovertible authority is conferred on a rule by using the word "established" in connection with it. The point of using this word is not to rule out departure from the convention but to indicate that such departure may need to be justified. On this view "Bachelors are male" would not be an analytic truth but only a partial definition. It is indeed true, but only in so far as it describes established word usage.

This view is not strong enough to license Ayer's conclusion that analytic truths depend upon "linguistic convention". A third form of conventionalism, since it represents any change in convention as itself a matter of convention, is strong enough to provide a basis for Ayer's conclusion, at least in some cases. For example, it is an analytic truth that (at the time of writing) one pound sterling is worth 240 pence. Decimalization involves a decision to change the convention upon which this truth depends. The change is wholly conventional, i.e. will not affect what the pound sterling is in fact worth. In token of this it is appropriate to say that it will be worth 100 *new* pence.

To the extent, indeed, that the correct use of a word may be subject to *stipulation*, a strong conventionalist account would seem to be warranted. But it would be wrong to suppose that the correct use of every expression is a matter for stipulation. This point may be brought out by reference to a contrast which may be drawn between the "legal" and the "social" use of the word "bachelor". In a legal context a bachelor is an unmarried man of marriageable age. Since this is a matter for stipulation, there is no provision possible for extension of the word's use. But in a social context considerations are applicable which license a narrower or broader use. We do not find it odd if people refuse the term "bachelor" to celibate priests. Our use of this and many other terms is affected by associations which make departures from established conventions possible. For example, the word "bachelor" is associated with a particular way of life which is thought appropriate for an unmarried man. Those who think this way of life no less appropriate for unmarried women may, without fear of self-contradiction, speak of "bachelor girls".

There may be other ways by which it may be possible to establish analytic truths. For example, "Red is a colour" seems to be such a truth of this kind which does not depend upon considerations of convention. That this is so seems to be because "red" is a wholly descriptive word. A change in the concept 'red' seems for this reason impossible. But it does not seem possible to rule out changes in the concepts in terms of which we understand our experience. In relation to explanatory terms, therefore, it does not seem possible to speak of analytic truths at all. Philosophers have not infrequently tried to defend grammatical propositions as though they were analytic in character. But this line of defence is not available for such propositions. They do indeed indicate "conventions" about word usage—but only in the weaker sense of the word "convention". They are not sanctioned by any convention. In their case the convention itself needs to be justified rather than simply appealed to.

What might be described as the "conventionalist move" has not uncommonly been made in relation to conceptual

changes in science. For those who propose conceptual changes
need to do so in terms in accordance with which what they
claim may *appear* to be absurd or self-contradictory. The
"conventionalist move" is to point out that this is so and to
insist that what is claimed is absurd or self-contradictory. An
example of this is to be found in Galileo's *Dialogue Concerning
the Two Chief World Systems.*[6]

One of the issues discussed is whether or not the Moon is
perfectly spherical. Simplicio, the defender of traditional views,
answers this question affirmatively. He is opposed by Salviati,
the Galilean spokesman in the *Dialogue*. Simplicio offers the
following argument in support of the position he adopts:

> Being ingenerable, incorruptible, inalterable, invariant, eternal,
> etc., implies that the celestial bodies are absolutely perfect; and
> being absolutely perfect entails their having all kinds of perfection.
> Therefore their shape is also perfect; that is to say, spherical; and
> absolutely and perfectly spherical, not approximately and
> irregularly (op. cit., p. 84).

Since the Moon is a celestial body, on Simplicio's account, it
becomes for him what might be termed an "analytic" matter
that the Moon is perfectly spherical. It would not otherwise be
a celestial body. When Sagredo undertakes to show that
"celestial bodies are no less generable and corruptible than
elemental", Simplicio makes the conventionalist move in
reply. To succeed in doing this, he retorts, would be to accom-
plish what is impossible (op. cit., p. 41). Any argument which
might appear to support such a conclusion is, in his opinion,
a "sophism".

From Simplicio's point of view, Sagredo and Salviati are
raising an "external question"[7] with regard to the idea of a
'celestial body'. Their understanding of such bodies as the

---

[6] tr. S. Drake, Berkeley and Los Angeles (University of California Press)
1953. The two "systems" are the Ptolemaic and the Copernican.

[7] Carnap, whose terminology I am here adopting, considers such questions
to be cognitively meaningless. To that extent he is committed to endorsing
the conventionalist move against *any* proposed conceptual change. On his
view, which I discuss in Section 29, such questions are to be construed as
practical questions about what linguistic framework to adopt.

Moon was different from that of Simplicio. One might say that they thought of the Moon as a *planetary* rather than a *celestial* body. But they used the language of the very view they were rejecting in order to express their rejection of it. Thus they *appeared* to be saying something absurd. The conventionalist move made by Simplicio, however, betrays his misunderstanding of their position. For their claim that the Moon was, *as a matter of fact*, not perfectly spherical presupposed a different understanding of the kind of body the Moon is.

It seems inappropriate to say that Sagredo and Salviati *simply opted* for a different convention. For then there would seem no ground for complaint against the conventionalist move. Simplicio's move, after all, does no more than to attempt to insist on the established convention. But what seems wrong about so construing the issue is that it misrepresents what is at stake. For what is at stake is which understanding of the kind of body the Moon is should be taken as the *right* one. It is true that the argument is somewhat at cross-purposes. But it does not follow from this that the issue is "merely verbal". On the contrary, questions of *truth* are clearly at stake in this case. For one party to the dispute contends that it is some kind of *necessary truth* that the Moon is perfectly spherical, whereas the other parties contend that it is a *contingent falsehood*. In claiming it to be contingently false that the Moon is perfectly spherical, one would be *committed* to denying that the Moon *must* be perfectly spherical. One is committed to denying one grammatical claim because one is committed to accepting another, in this case the claim that the Moon *may* be other than perfectly spherical. If this is so, then grammatical claims are non-definitionally true[8] and cannot be construed merely as proposals for different linguistic conventions.

[8] There are considerable difficulties which must be met by such an account. I shall try to meet them in Section 20.

12. INSIGHT AND UNDERSTANDING

The kind of more adequate understanding which might be claimed in the two examples of conceptual change given might be said to involve what is commonly called "insight". For what is involved in such cases is not so much the recognition of facts not previously accepted as such. It is more like seeing matters in a new light. This may lead to, but does not consist in, the acquisition of further information about matters of fact. In adopting the term "insight", however, I shall use it within more confined limits than those reflected in its ordinary usage. My use of this term will be confined to a class of true grammatical claims. This class may be identified informally[9] by saying that it is a mark of an "insight" that coming to understand it and seeing that it is true are indistinguishable. The dichotomy between understanding a claim and recognizing it as true applies to matter-of-fact, but not to grammatical, claims. The short explanation[10] of why this is so is that coming to understand a grammatical claim involves a change in the concepts one has.

To see a claim as one of "insight" we need to inform it with two different backgrounds in relation to each of which it may be seen as having a different standing in grammar. For example, the claim that the Earth influences the Moon can be regarded as involving an insight, namely, that the Earth *can* influence the Moon. In relation to Ptolemaic astronomy it makes no sense to suppose such a possibility. But given the understanding of the kind of body the Moon is which has prevailed in subsequent scientific theory it has become possible to regard it as true—as a matter of fact—that the Earth does influence the Moon. If we do not find it natural to regard such a claim as embodying any insight this may be attributed to the distance which history has placed between us and the contemporaries

[9] More formal treatment of the notion of 'insight' is deferred to Section 30.

[10] A fuller explanation is offered in Section 25.

of Galileo. It requires some imagination in us if we are to understand how it could have been supposed impossible for the Earth to have any effect upon the Moon.

For reasons which should become apparent, it is wrong for a philosopher to suppose that it lies within his province to assess the merit of all claims to insight whatever. But there are cases in which, if only by tradition, philosophers have become particularly interested. These are cases in which the adequacy of certain concepts of philosophical concern is at stake. One of these is the concept 'hypocrisy' in so far as a satisfactory account of it depends upon a satisfactory account of sincerity.

It is commonly supposed that a hypocrite is someone whose insincerity takes the form of trying to take other people in with regard to his motive for doing certain things. This view finds philosophical expression in Gibbert Ryle's treatment of hypocrisy in *The Concept of Mind*.[11] On Ryle's account, hypocrisy stands to motives much as charlatanry stands to abilities. To be hypocritical is "to try to appear actuated by a motive other than one's real motive". Just as the charlatan must be artful in order to succeed in pretending to have abilities he does not have, so the hypocrite must master certain "tricks" in order to pass off his shammed motive as the real one. For such an understanding of hypocrisy the studied humility of Dicken's character Uriah Heep serves as a good example.

The term "hypocrite" is indeed well-entrenched in our language as a term of moral abuse. Hypocrisy is firmly connected with insincerity. And it is tempting to assimilate all cases of insincerity to the clearest kind of case, namely, that involved in lying. But it might be questioned whether all cases of insincerity *must* take the form of self-conscious deception. In particular it might be doubted whether the insincerity of the hypocrite should be understood in the way appropriate to that of the liar. Dietrich Bonhoeffer writes that the hypocrite will "suppose himself to be the one who is acting genuinely and

[11] London (Hutchinson) 1949, p. 172f. and New York (Barnes & Noble) 1950.

cannot but utterly reject the reproach of hypocrisy".[12] The theologian Mozley once remarked:[13] "Who is to convert the hypocrite? He does not know he is a hypocrite. . . . The greater hypocrite he is, the more sincere he must think himself." Neither of these remarks can be said to *make sense* in terms of that widely accepted view of hypocrisy which finds expression in Ryle's book. Indeed, in so far as Bonhoeffer and Mozley seem to be trying to say something different about hypocrisy, we might say that it is part of the point of putting their remarks in the way in which they do that there should be an apparent unintelligibility about them.

But expressions of genuine insight share this apparent unintelligibility with various unacceptable claims to insight, including pseudo-insights. The question is whether or not they introduce us to a more adequate concept of hypocrisy—or a better understanding of it—than that afforded by the terms in relation to which they do not make sense. The answer is, I think, affirmative. For such remarks remind us of the way in which self-deception can quite characteristically feature in cases of hypocrisy. In doing so, they highlight the fact that there are more subtle and less blatant forms which insincerity may take than that involved in lying. There have indeed been accounts of self-deception which represent it as involving a man setting about inducing a false belief in himself much as he might in deceiving someone else. But the difficulty with such accounts is that the only terms on which such a programme could be carried out do not allow the self-deceiver to be aware of his success. For were he so aware he would thereby recognize his belief to be a false one and cease to hold it. It seems more appropriate to regard self-deception as a product of wishful thinking. Where the hypocrite is guilty of self-deception he may, on such an account, be unaware—or at any rate largely unaware—of his true motives. To the extent that there is a

---

[12] *Ethics*, tr. N. H. Smith, London (SCM Press) 1955, Fontana Edition 1964, p. 168.

[13] *University Sermons* ii 34, quoted from the entry under "Hypocrite" in the *Oxford English Dictionary* (1901).

culpable lack of integrity about the way in which he behaves, the hypocrite may still be regarded as "insincere".

If one accepts such an account of hypocrisy and insincerity one will be prepared to say that the hypocrite will sometimes regard himself as sincere. One will thus be committed to accepting the grammatical claim that the hypocrite *may* think of himself as sincere and to rejecting the incompatible grammatical claim that the hypocrite *must* think of himself as *in*sincere. The conceptual disagreement about how to account for hypocrisy and insincerity is reflected at a matter-of-fact level. For if one accepts one account one will be prepared to count as true or false as a matter of fact the claim that a given hypocrite regards himself as sincere. If one accepts the other account this possibility is precluded. There is a sense, as will later be argued,[14] in which the possibility of any matter-of-fact claim being made depends upon the *truth* of some grammatical claim. But it is sufficient to note here that there could be no question of its being either true or false that a given hypocrite regards himself as sincere (or insincere) if this were not permitted by the grammar of acceptable talk about hypocrisy. The acceptability of speaking in one way rather than another may be a matter for contention. But there is nothing sacrosanct about accepted grammar. The error involved in "conventionalist moves" is to suppose that only accepted grammar is acceptable.

This is not to say that considerable justification may not be given for being cautious in relation to proposed conceptual changes. For they may embody only partial insights or indeed no insight at all. Neglect of accepted grammar may indeed give rise to pseudo-insights. A childish example would be where a man says to himself: "But the flame *must* go somewhere when it goes out!"

It is not difficult to find cases where philosophers have been led into error through neglect of grammar. This seems to be true of Descartes, as was indicated in the previous chapter. But not all departures from accepted grammar involve

[14] See Section 20 below.

grammatical "mistakes". On the contrary, it does seem possible to *justify* a change in grammar. This possibility has implications which bear on the epistemological standing of religious affirmations. These implications will be considered at a later stage.

V

BELIEF AND CONCEPTUAL CHANGE

IT HAS been argued, in Chapter III, that religious assertions cannot be dismissed holus-bolus as unintelligible by quite general standards of intelligibility, since it has not been shown that there are such standards.[1] On the contrary, it has been argued, there is reason to believe that the standards by which such assertions should be judged are implicit in the language of religion. This would, however, only be so if the language of religion could be shown to be distinctive. And it has been suggested that the standards to which religious assertions are subject are those which prevail in the society within which those assertions are made. Hence, while religious claims may at one time have been intelligible to members of a given society, it is possible for them to cease to be so at a later date.

Two kinds of thesis are prompted by this consideration. Like U-theses and R-theses, they may share a common base. And like U-theses and R-theses, they adopt respectively contrasting positions as to whether the intelligibility of some piece of discourse is something which can be salvaged. The common base can, in this case, only be expressed rather vaguely by saying that religious assertions are subject to the standards of intelligibility which prevail in a given culture. According to the C-thesis, the claims of religion were once, but are no longer, intelligible by those standards. According to the D-thesis, this is so, but not irredeemably so. The D-thesis advocates a programme of translation into the modern idiom

[1] I shall qualify this remark somewhat in the next chapter, to allow for certain formal conditions as binding on all statement-making discourse. But these qualifications do not affect the discussion here.

which is designed to restore the intelligibility of religious claims.

The prior question, whether or not religion does embody standards of what it makes sense to say within itself, has formed the substance of a current controversy amongst theologians. The issue has overtly been one about the nature of modern Biblical theology. But, since it seems to turn on epistemological rather than theological considerations, I shall presume to address myself to it also in this chapter.

13. TWO VIEWS OF BIBLICAL THEOLOGY

Theologians have, in recent years, been much concerned with the question whether or not the terms in which the Christian faith is to be presented should be drawn from a contemporary secular understanding of the world or whether it can only be understood in its own terms. Rudolf Bultmann is noted for his advocacy of the view that exegesis of the Bible cannot be free of "secular conceptions". He thinks, on the contrary, that every interpreter is "inescapably dependent on conceptions which he has inherited from a tradition" (JCM 54). And, since "every tradition is dependent on some philosophy or other", his option is restricted to that contemporary philosophy which is best suited to express the claims of the Christian religion. Bultmann himself attempts this task in terms drawn from Heidegger's existentialism. But it is in taking "the modern world-view" as "the criterion of the Scripture and the Christian message" that he commits himself to a D-thesis. For he recognizes that he must adopt the position that "Scripture and the Christian message are not allowed to say anything that is in contradiction with the modern world-view" (JCM 35).

This view has been repudiated by Karl Barth in the name of the autonomy of theology. He declares it to be one of his chief aims

> to emancipate understanding, both of the Bible and things in general, from the Egyptian bondage in which one philosophy after another had tried to take control and teach us what the Holy Spirit was allowed to say... (KM II 127).

While Barth does not reject the influence of philosophy altogether, he considers it a "corruption of theology" to treat it as though it were "a branch of general mental science". It has, he claims, its own rules and standards which should not be confused with those of other disciplines. Only a "bungler" would attempt to invoke as a "final standard" what has been gleaned from "this or that logic or ontology or psychology or sociology". Dogmatics, like other disciplines, "has and must have its own language".[2] Its decisive criterion is the Bible. Though the theologian cannot be indifferent to what Barth calls "the culture problem" (what I have been calling "the intelligibility gap"), he must not allow his criteria to be affected by his desire to overcome it. For Barth, the problem of communicating the claims of religion to the secular world is a separate problem from those faced by the theologian in trying to understand the Bible.[3]

On this point Barth and Bultmann are directly opposed to one another. For, in Bultmann's view, the theologian cannot, without dishonesty, regard the removal of the out-dated elements of the Bible as a different enterprise from his making the claims of the Bible intelligible to himself. He is, after all, no less a modern man than his secular contemporaries. Such out-dated conceptions as involve speaking of heaven as "above" the earth or hell as "beneath" it have, according to Bultmann, "lost all meaning". Nor do they become any the more meaningful to a man by virtue of his becoming religious. On Barth's view, on the other hand, it is necessary to learn the language of the Church if one is to understand its teaching. On his view, understanding is itself a gift of divine grace.

Barth's view, that the language of the "community of faith" has its own standards internal to itself has, not surprisingly,

[2] This is the branch of theology concerned with the statement of doctrine. Barth's view is forcefully stated in his *Church Dogmatics*, (tr. G. T. Thomson), Edinburgh (T. & T. Clark) 1936.

[3] As he himself puts it: "The task of translation is a secondary concern, and it can only be done well if both reader and exegete take in hand the primary task first." (KM II 88).

been developed along Wittgensteinian lines. W. Hordern,[4] for example, has claimed that theology is a "language-game" with distinctive rules of its own.[5] It is thus subject to standards of criticism internal to itself and cannot, without distortion, be subjected to external standards. Such a view accords with that of Barth over against that of Bultmann.

14. THE PROBLEM ABOUT MYTHOLOGY

It has become widely recognized in religious circles that the men of the Bible and the early Church had a very different outlook on the world from that which we have today. Some have thought that these men were more aware of the presence of God and that we should therefore try to recover their outlook. Others, however, have thought that it was not merely *undesirable* that we should attempt to recover this outlook, but that it was in some way no longer *open* for us to do so. There is, it is said, a good deal in that outlook which is simply no longer intelligible to modern men. This claim is part of what is involved in the suggestion that the Christian message, as presented in the New Testament, is embedded in a "mythical" or "mythological" framework. It has been advocated by Rudolf Bultmann in his well-known paper "New Testament and Mythology" (KM I), where he argues that these "mythological" elements in the Christian message need to be removed. The essential message can, he thinks, still be preserved intact, for there is nothing "specifically Christian" about this framework as such. A process of *de*-mythologizing, it is thought, can restore the intelligibility of the claims of Christianity.

Bultmann is, as I shall try to bring out, committed to a

---

[4] In his *Speaking of God: the Nature and Purpose of Theological Language*, New York (Macmillan) 1964, p. 83f.

[5] Wittgenstein does not seem to use the term "language-game" in such a large way. But the thought seems to be the same. For example, Wittgenstein, in his *Lectures on Religious Belief*, remarked: "Whether a thing is a blunder or not—it is a blunder in a particular system. Just as something is a blunder in a particular game and not in another." See *Wittgenstein: Lectures and Conversations* (ed. C. Barrett), Oxford (Blackwell) 1966, p. 59.

D-thesis, founded on the claim (shared with C-theses) that the standards of intelligibility to which religious claims are subject are those prevailing in society at large. His position is further characterized, and thereby distinguished from a C-thesis, by his view that religious claims can be made intelligible in terms which conform to those prevailing standards. But he is at least not fully aware of his commitment to a D-thesis and may indeed have slipped into it by error. For he considers the intelligibility gap to be due to the presentation of the Christian religion in terms of the "cosmology of a pre-scientific age". This creates a barrier for modern understanding, since such a manner of presentation confers on religious claims a pseudo-scientific character. Thus they appear, on the face of it, to have the unacceptable character of out-worn superstitions.

> Myth is an expression of man's conviction that the origin and purpose of the world in which he lives are to be sought not within it but beyond it—that is, beyond the realm of known and tangible reality—and that this realm is perpetually dominated and menaced by those powers which are its source and limit (KM I 10f.).

It is in these terms that Bultmann introduces the notion of 'myth'. Divine transcendence, for example, is represented in "mythological" terms by spatial distance. Heaven is seen as being "above" the earth and Hell as "beneath" it. The presence of evil is represented by demons or evil spirits which may occupy places or persons. The world is largely in the control of "principalities and powers". What order it displays is due to Jehovah's supremacy over these lesser powers.

The "mythological" view of the world is thus presented in sharp opposition to that suggested by modern science. We cannot now believe, he says, that Heaven is *literally* "above" the earth, that stars do or ever did actually stand still above particular places, that men or places may be inhabited by demons, or that the faithful will rise to meet the Son of Man in the air. Now that we understand the world better, we can see that its regularities can be accounted for in terms of natural laws. No room is left in our understanding for supernatural

interruptions of those regularities. It is characteristic of the
"mythological" world-view to be "open" to the possibility of
this kind of intrusion. But no such possibility can be contemplated within the view of the world adopted in science.

A re-interpretation of the Christian message is therefore
needed. And the key to such a re-interpretation lies, Bultmann
thinks, in understanding the "real purpose" of myth. For though
myth makes an "apparent claim to objective validity", its *real
purpose* is

> not to present an objective picture of the world as it is, but to
> express man's understanding of himself in the world in which he
> lives. Myth should be interpreted not cosmologically, but anthro-
> pologically, or better still, existentially (KM I 10).

Bultmann's distinction between the "apparent" and the "real"
purpose of myth is not supported by much argument. It seems,
indeed, that his primary consideration in drawing it is to
underline the need for some programme of de-mythologizing.
For he wishes to say *both* that myth does express something of
importance *and* that, taken at its face-value, it is quite unacceptable. What truth there is, in speaking of Heaven above
the earth, cannot lie in its merits as a contribution to astronomy.
The spatial language is intended to express something deeper,
which would become more apparent if the spatial language
were dispensed with altogether.

It may seem that this line of argument leads on naturally to
the view that the mythological elements of the Bible are to be
understood allegorically. Thus Heaven would be understood as
spiritually superior to the earth, or something like that. And
certainly Bultmann's scepticism about finding anything much
of historical fact in the New Testament has led some of his
critics to attribute such a position to him. But he seems aware
of the dangers in trying to represent myth as *simply* a pic-
turesque if misleading way of expressing truths about the human
condition. Thus, even though he thinks the crucifixion story
needs to be radically de-mythologized, he still wishes to speak
of "the decisive act of God in Christ". He wishes, that is to say,
to speak of realities which lie beyond what can be empirically

ascertained. His bold use of words like "fact" and "situation" in the following passage make this clear:

> This interpretation of the cross as *a permanent fact* rather than a mythological event does far more justice to the redemptive significance of the event of the past than do the traditional interpretations. In the last resort mythological language is *only a medium for conveying the meaning of the past event*. The real meaning of the cross is that it has created a new and *permanent situation* in history (KM I 37, italics mine).

While, however, it may be Bultmann's *intention* to retain the distinctively factual content of the Christian message, it is by no means clear that he has provided himself with the terms in which this would be possible. It seems, on the contrary, that he is committed by the terms of his de-mythologizing programme to construing the Christian religion in a wholly secular way. It seems indeed that his failure sufficiently to realize the radical direction in which such a programme pulls him is due, at least in part, to mistaken assumptions of an epistemological kind. He supposes, in the first place, that he is doing no more than re-expressing the claims of the Christian religion in terms of a more acceptable *world-view*. But, as I shall bring out in the next section, he is misled by the vagueness of the idea of a 'world-view' into confusing cosmological with epistemological theses.

His second mistaken assumption arises in direct consequence of this. He takes it for granted that there ought, in principle, to be no problem in *explaining* the Christian message to the unbeliever. He assumes, that is to say, that the "eye of faith" is needed only to believe the claims of religion, not to understand them. Bultmann accepts that "what we call facts of redemption are themselves objects of faith and are apprehended as such only by the eye of faith" (JCM 72). But we do not need faith, on this view, to make sense of the claims of religion. This is one major issue between a D-thesis and a B-thesis about religious claims. For the former thesis presents the intelligibility gap as a fortuitous one, to be eliminated by a programme of translation into the modern idiom, whereas the latter thesis represents it as an inevitable feature of the situation between believer and unbeliever.

Mistaken or not, however, this second epistemological assumption of Bultmann's follows from the first. It follows, that is to say, from his regarding the issue as one about "world-views" rather than "conceptions of reality". But, if a distinction *must* be made between "world-views" and "conceptions of reality" and if it is in terms of a secular conception of reality that Bultmann is committed to presenting the claims of religion, then his thesis cannot succeed. For, as has been brought out in discussion of reductionism, identity of belief cannot be preserved between two different conceptions of reality in so far as they are different. It follows, then, that if there is an intelligibility gap, it cannot be bridged by any programme of re-interpretation.

15. "WORLD-VIEWS" AND "CONCEPTIONS OF REALITY"

It is a feature of a *myth*, on Bultmann's view, that it represents "transcendent reality" in terms of "an immanent, this-worldly objectivity" (JCM 19). In other words, it speaks of the divine in cosmological terms. The clearest example of this is the three-decker universe with the world in the middle, Heaven above and Hell beneath. It is not difficult to see what is meant by describing this as a "world-view" at odds with any non-geocentric cosmology. Had Bultmann confined his use of the notion of a 'world-view' to such cases, his position would have been clear enough. But it would not, for connected reasons, have been sufficiently far-reaching. For he wishes to speak of talk about supernatural powers as called in question not so much by "the concrete results of scientific research and the contents of a world-view", but by "the method of thinking from which world-views follow" (JCM 37). Belief in the operation of supernatural powers—a feature of the "mythological world-view"—is not expressly ruled out by scientific theory. It is, however, excluded by the attitudes of mind which are appropriate to scientific inquiry.

Bultmann is thus quickly led into contrasting "the ancient world-view" and "the modern world-view" as "two ways of thinking" (JCM 38). The notion of a 'world-view' is stretched so that it applies not merely to cosmological beliefs but to attitudes of mind. He goes on to speak of the rejection of the miraculous as one feature of "the modern world-view" which marks it as modern:

> ... modern man acknowledges as reality only such phenomena or events as are comprehensible within the framework of the rational order of the universe. He does not acknowledge miracles because they do not fit into this lawful order. When a strange or marvellous accident occurs, he does not rest until he has found a rational cause (JCM 37f.).

For Bultmann, the modern "world-view" is "closed" to the possibility of such supernatural interruptions of the natural course of events. There is, in other words, nothing which would *count* for someone who saw the world this way as a "miraculous" event. And this, as we have seen, is another way of saying that the notion of a 'miracle' is *unintelligible* to such a person.

It is in this way that Bultmann's position, almost inadvertently, takes on an epistemological character. The notion of a 'world-view' is extended in such a way that its application to cosmologies appears superficial. But, it might be thought, it would not matter if wholly secular standards of intelligibility were endorsed with regard to what many regard as peripheral issues, such as demon-possession or miracles. Bultmann's programme, however, is too thorough-going to stop at pruning off some aspects of traditional belief which it is not necessary for faith to insist upon. For his notion of 'myth' is itself affected by his epistemological commitments. He seems, at points, almost to say that a claim is "mythological" in so far as it contains any quasi-factual claim over and above what would nowadays be found intelligible as a factual claim. This seems his position in his treatment of the traditional claim that Jesus of Nazareth was crucified, dead and buried, that he descended into Hell, and that he rose again from the dead to sit at the right hand of God.

Bultmann departs radically from those apologists who have claimed that the resurrection of Jesus is "the best-attested fact in history", as it is commonly put. He does not even think that the resurrection is a historical fact *at all*. For, on his interpretation, "the cross and the resurrection form an indivisible cosmic event" (KM I 38). The death of Jesus can, he suggests, be viewed *either* historically, as no more than the death of a religious teacher, *or*, through the "eye of faith", as the salvation of mankind. These are, he insists, two ways—but distinct ways—of apprehending the same event. To bring this point out, he makes use of a distinction recognized in the German (though not the English) language. It is between a *historisch* (usually translated "historical") event and a *geschichtlich* (usually translated "historic") event. The death of Jesus may be considered either as a "historical" (*historisch*) event, that is to say, as a bare fact of (secular) history. Or it may be considered as *something more* than this, including the significance which attaches to it. The death of Jesus may thus be considered as a "historic" (*geschichtlich*) event. It is indeed this "historic" aspect which is conveyed by the mythological language in which Jesus' death is described in the New Testament. So considered, it may be seen as an act of atonement.

What is noteworthy about this account is Bultmann's acceptance of the criteria used by secular historians for deciding what will count as a past event. He is *not* saying that the atonement is more than an event of the past (which would be the orthodox claim) but that the atonement is not itself a past event. It is rather, on his account, the permanent significance of a past event. But its significance consists only in what *we* may attach to the event. Thus the crucifixion signifies for us, he seems to be saying, the possibility of authentic human existence. But it is not clear what, more than an imagined, connection can be claimed for the relation between the crucifixion and such a possibility. What is it, we may wonder, for us to see this event as having this significance? Bultmann does not provide a steady answer to this question.

Indeed, his quandary seems to be a consequence of his

wishing to hold both to orthodoxy and to the need for a de-mythologizing programme. For he wishes both to say that religion speaks to us of "invisible, intangible realities" (KM I 113) and also to accept a framework within which such realities cannot be intelligibly spoken of. He thus runs into an objection voided by C. Wehrung[6] that

> *while orthodoxy as a whole* speaks of an event which can be objectively established . . . something which happens, and remains outside of us, to which faith is related, Bultmann—and this is something which he has very much at heart—relates the event so exclusively to faith that faith absorbs it entirely.

It is not Bultmann's intention to reduce God's action to "a purely subjective, psychological experience (*Erlebnis*)" (JCM 70). But he does not provide himself with the terms in which he can speak intelligibly of such action. For his across-the-board programme of de-mythologizing points to dispensing with religious facts as such altogether.

Bultmann is, as have been other advocates of D-theses, excessively optimistic about the prospect of retaining identity of belief between what was accepted in "mythological" terms and what is accepted in de-mythologized terms. He assumes, as others[7] have done, that there is a *central core* of Christian belief which may be preserved despite radical alterations in the terms in which it is wrapped. But recognizing two claims as being expressions of the same belief involves knowing what it would be for both of them to be true. And this in turn is only possible for a man who embraces a conception of reality within which he can make sense of both claims.

It is just at this point, however, that D-theses run into a difficulty. For their advocates must admit to *not* knowing what it is for one side—that expressed in "mythological" terms—to be

[6] Quoted by L. Malavez in his *The Christian Message and Myth*, tr. O. Wyon, London (SCM Press) 1958, p. 67.

[7] See J. A. T. Robinson's *Honest to God*, London (SCM Press) and Philadelphia (Westminster Press) 1963, p. 124. Robinson says that what is needed is "a radically new mould or *meta-morphosis* of Christian belief and practice". He is convinced that such a recasting will "leave the fundamental truth of the Gospel unaffected", but offers no reason for supposing that it will.

true. But if they admit *that*, then they are in no position to offer a re-interpretation in non-mythological terms. Yet if they insist they *are* in such a position, then the basis on which their programme is claimed to be necessary is undermined. For they themselves are members of the culture in whose terms the "mythological" claims were supposed to be unintelligible. But how could that be true if they themselves are able to understand them? Barth criticizes Bultmann on just this score:

> Apparently he [Bultmann] already knows *what* is in the New Testament [sc. "prior to beginning his programme"]. Apparently that is why he wants himself and he wants us to concentrate entirely on translating it from one language and one set of terms into others. For we already know what it is we are trying to translate (KM II 88).

In making this criticism, Barth draws attention to the comparative advantage enjoyed by his position in this respect.

The D-thesis is open, then, to a paradox which is very similar to that which arises for strict reductionist theses. There are, however, two important differences. R-theses are based on standards which are held to be universally valid for all time, whereas D-theses are based on standards which are binding only on a particular culture at a particular time. Moreover, the paradox of reductionism can be avoided by someone advocating an R-thesis who does not pretend to offer an interpretation which preserves identity of belief. This option, however, could scarcely commend itself to Bultmann. For it would make his position as loosely related to traditional Christianity as is that of Feuerbach. And he has repudiated suggestions by critics who have claimed that this is just where he does stand.

This is not to say that a partial programme of de-mythologizing might not be admissible. My arguments have been directed against it as an *across-the-board programme*. They do not rule out simply pruning off certain aspects of the Biblical conception of reality as not essential to religious belief. But it would, of course, be a theological matter which aspects these might be. One example, however, which has often been put forward, may be sufficiently uncontroversial to make the point.

It has been said not uncommonly that we should now understand demon-possession in terms of madness. Something like a revised D-thesis might be involved in so construing demon-possession. But, in being a suitably revised form of D-thesis, it does not embody a claim to preserve identity of belief. Yet, given that this is only a peripheral matter, it might be argued that no basic belief is compromised by accepting it. Whether there would be much point in such a partial form of D-thesis is another matter.

I have suggested that Bultmann's difficulty derives in part from the epistemological commitments of his use of the notion of 'myth'. Ironically, indeed, his way of presenting the "mythological world-view" has the effect of making it appear comparatively modern. For it is by reference to a modern secular conception of reality that a myth is to be identified as such. In consequence, such descriptions as that of pretending "to present an objective view of the world as it is" (KM I 10) say more about that modern conception of reality than they do about the "world-view" Bultmann is trying to characterize.

In his use of the notion of myth Bultmann adopts what has been, at any rate until quite recently, a common practice of anthropologists. That is to make it a criterion of something's being a "myth" that there should be no question of its being true. Malinowski, for example,[8] insists on the importance of myth as a cultural force, but nevertheless rules out, at least by implication, the possibility of a myth's being true:

> The myth assists primitive man in situations of emotional distress and at the crises of life. It shows a way out when there is no empirically obvious way out. The eternal truths of religion are indispensable *pragmatic figments* without which civilization cannot survive (My italics).

Malinowski's attempt to state *the real function* of myth is strongly reminiscent of Bultmann's attempt to declare its *real purpose*. In both cases it is the notion of myth used which makes

[8] *Myth in Primitive Psychology*, London (Kegan Paul, Trench, Trubner & Co.) 1926, p. 23ff. I am indebted to Winch's book *The Idea of a Social Science*, London (Routledge & Kegan Paul) 1958 for the line of thought which my point here exemplifies.

the apparent *v* actual (purpose or function) distinction seem to be necessary. And the hazards for the study of anthropology are just as severe as are posed for exegesis. For the way in which Malinowski closes the door on the possibility of "the eternal truths" of religion being *truths* jeopardizes the very inquiry in which he professes to be engaged. If the anthropologist takes his own conception of reality as the criterion for identifying a myth as such, then his study, in so far as it purports to be a study of the beliefs held by primitive peoples, will be marred by reflecting his own outlook too much. It is in danger of providing more understanding of the anthropologist's own society than that of the society he is engaged in examining.

It may seem that my arguments lend support to more conservative views of Biblical exegesis. For such views do lay considerable emphasis on construing the claims of the Bible in the way intended by their authors. J. I. Packer,[9] for example, expresses such a conservative position in the following terms:

> . . . when Scripture professes to narrate fact, faith receives the narrative as factual on God's authority, and does not conclude it to be legendary, or mythical, or mistaken, on mere human authority.

But to construe the claims of the Bible as stating "literal fact" is to make what is in essence the very same mistake as that of Bultmann. For it is *our* notion of 'literal fact' which is being employed in interpreting the Biblical claims. Once again there is the problem of projecting a contemporary conception of reality on to those claims. For what may be professed as fact can only be received *by us* as fact if we share a common conception of reality with those who have made the profession. And it is precisely this assumption, made by Packer, which cannot be made.

It does not, of course, follow from Bultmann's position being untenable that the opposing view of Barth is correct. No inconsistency would be involved in supposing both views to be untenable. To show that Barth is right over against Bultmann

[9] *'Fundamentalism' and the Word of God*, London (Inter-Varsity Fellowship) 1958, p. 167 fn.

on this issue, one would need to establish some form of B-thesis. And, though some considerations have been offered which would support such a thesis, it would be premature to suppose it to have been established.

16. SECULARIZATION AND CONCEPTUAL CHANGE

A. C. MacIntyre, in presenting a form of C-thesis, shows himself to be keenly aware of just those difficulties which face exegetes like Bultmann and anthropologists like Malinowski. These difficulties he presents in the form of a dilemma. On the one hand, "to make a belief and the concepts it embodies intelligible I cannot avoid invoking my own criteria [sc. "of intelligibility"], or rather the established criteria of my own society" (FP 125). I cannot avoid doing this, since only on these terms can *I* come to an understanding of such a belief. For my understanding is limited by the standards which prevail in my society. On the other hand, if I bring those standards to bear upon what I see of other societies, there is a serious danger of my distorting the beliefs and practices of those societies. In doing this, I should be in danger of projecting on to my studies, as Frazer did, an image of the life of my own society. I cannot, it seems, understand without distorting: yet what I distort, I cannot fully understand.

Another aspect of this dilemma emerges from our coming to such a study with fixed standards of intelligibility which we have absorbed in growing up in and learning the language of our own society. On the one hand, we are in danger of treating those standards as universally valid. If we do this, we shall not begin to *understand* the beliefs and practices of other societies. To avoid this we must, according to MacIntyre, *begin* by "detecting the standards of intelligibility established in a society" (FP 126). There is, however, a danger of over-reacting against "the metaphysical fiction of one over-all 'norm for intelligibility in general'" by "flying to a total relativism" (FP 120) which precludes the possibility of external criticism of the beliefs held in a society. He quotes the following passage from Winch's book[10] in support of attributing such a relativist position to him:

> . . . criteria of logic are not a direct gift of God, but arise out of, and are only intelligible in the context of, ways of living or modes of social life as such. For instance, science is one such mode and religion is another; and each has criteria of intelligibility peculiar to itself. So within science or religion actions may be logical or illogical; in science, for example, it would be illogical to refuse to be bound by the results of a properly carried out experiment; in religion it would be illogical to suppose that one could pit one's strength against God's; and so on. But we cannot sensibly say that either the practice of science or that of religion is either illogical or logical; both are non-logical.

MacIntyre rejects this view since he holds that "sometimes to understand a concept involves not sharing it". This is so where the concept itself is incoherent. We need then an account of its incoherence which does justice to its use in a given society together with an account which brings out how members of that society have failed to reject the concept as incoherent. One kind of case is where the incoherence of a concept is not realized by members of society until they are obliged to ask certain questions of themselves. MacIntyre suggests this is so with the concept of the divine right of kings. This concept seemed satisfactory until rival claimants to the throne appeared on the scene. The question was then posed: "Which king has the divine right?" And this question exposed an incoherence in the concept. Another kind of case is where the incoherence is to some extent manifest to users of the concept, but where "the use of the concept is so intimately bound up with forms of description which cannot be dispensed with if social and intellectual life is to continue that any device for putting up with the incoherence is more tolerable than dispensing with the concept" (FP 127).

10 *The Idea of a Social Science*, p. 100f. Those familiar with the published discussion between MacIntyre and Winch will recognize my indebtedness to it. For reasons connected largely with the complexity of the issues between them, I have avoided any attempt to contribute directly to that discussion. As the question of relativism arises in relation to the B-thesis, I shall, however, discuss it below, in Section 20.

This is, according to MacIntyre, the position of medieval Christianity. Its concepts were incoherent, but were suffered as involving what were called "paradoxes" because of their place in medieval thought and life. But for us to understand the Christian religion is, he claims, incompatible with *our* believing it. For it "has lost the social context which once made it comprehensible" (FP 132). An understanding of that context enables us to grasp the rules which govern the use of those concepts, but, in doing so, we come to see that they cannot be used intelligibly.

MacIntyre speaks of "invoking *our* standards" in detecting incoherence of this kind (FP 126). But this seems to conflict with what he says elsewhere, where it is expressly allowed that a man may come to recognize the incoherence of certain beliefs and practices which are established *in his own society* (FP 121f.). This would suggest, and it would seem to be MacIntyre's considered opinion,[11] that not contradicting oneself is on a different footing from other standards of intelligibility. It is not, that is to say, *our* standards in particular that are being *invoked* when the criticism of incoherence is made, but quite formal and therefore general standards binding on all discourse.

How then, if at all, are *our* standards *invoked* (i.e. *appealed to*) in attempting to understand the beliefs and practices of primitive peoples? In what way are we, as members of a particular society, subject to "cultural limitations" of a kind which restrict what we can attach sense to? MacIntyre says little which would provide a direct answer to these questions. But his thought seems to be indicated by his concern to give an account which will accommodate what I have described as "conceptual change". Thus he criticizes R. B. Braithwaite[12] for not allowing for the case where a man gives up religious belief "on the grounds that he can no longer find a sense" in

[11] In an unpublished paper, he makes this clear. I shall discuss the question of *formal* conditions of intelligibility in the following chapter.

[12] *An Empiricist's View of the Nature of Religious Belief*, Cambridge and New York (CUP) 1955. Braithwaite puts forward a form of P-thesis.

religious utterances (FP 125). He also criticizes Winch on the
ground that provision needs to be made for people calling in
question "the standards of intelligibility and rationality which
they have held hitherto" (FP 122). It seems indeed to be
conceptual change in the form of what MacIntyre calls "the
secularization of our forms of description" which leaves the
contradictions involved in Christian belief "high and dry".
This is brought out by the example he gives:

> . . . Christianity does not and never has depended upon the truth
> of an Aristotelian physics in which the physical system requires a
> Prime Mover, and consequently many sceptics as well as many
> believers have treated the destruction of the Aristotelian argument
> in its Thomist form as something very little germane to the ques-
> tion of whether or not Christianity is true. But in fact the replace-
> ment of a physics which requires a Prime Mover by a physics
> which does not secularizes a whole area of enquiry. It weakens the
> hold of the concept of God on our intellectual life by showing that
> in this area we can dispense with descriptions which have any con-
> nection with the concept (FP 129).

In this example, it is a change in the concept of motion
which makes possible the rejection of a premiss in the Thomist
argument, namely, that for something to move there is required
something which moves it. Physics, at least since Descartes,
has made use of a paradigm of motion which dispenses with
that of Aristotle. But what this shows is that *one* line of apologetic argument, designed to show that *we* cannot make sense
of the world without supposing there to be a God, no longer has
the force it might once have had. The *possibility*, assuming
that no such argument can now rationally impress us, of a
wholly secular conception of reality does not of itself show that
religious belief is no longer intelligible. Nor does MacIntyre
suppose it does. But he does seem to think that, given such
"secularization of our forms of description", what was formerly
taken to be a paradox is now exposed for what it is, namely, a
contradiction. Yet it is by no means clear *why* this should be
thought to follow.

The weight of MacIntyre's argument seems to lie on a thesis
which he shares with Bultmann. It is that religious persons are

subject in what they claim or believe to those norms of intelligibility which prevail in society at large. Up to the seventeenth century, he claims, we should all have been believers with no thought of being else. But, since then, "even for those who believe, the truth and intelligibility of their beliefs is not obvious in the same sense" (FP 128). He speaks also of "the appropriateness of scientific criteria from our standpoint" (FP 121). Just as the possibility of religious belief a few centuries ago was provided by a social context, so should our difficulties in finding it intelligible today be referred to our social context.

What does MacIntyre mean by a "social context"? It seems to be this, that it is by sharing in the same way of life that we are able to make sense of what other members of our society say and do. If a man holds out his hand to us in a certain way, we recognize that he wishes to shake hands with us and that this is a gesture of friendship. Now this might be taken to suggest that the shared standards of intelligibility are purely conventional. For we should have little difficulty in adjusting ourselves to other gestures which, in societies other than our own, serve the same purpose. There are, indeed, deviations in our own society. For while it is in general the right hand that is extended in friendship, Boy Scouts extend the left hand to one another, in token perhaps of the particular bond which unites them as members of that organization. But there are more difficult cases, where learning the convention is not enough to enable one to make sense of a piece of behaviour. One such case would be that of a minister of religion "pronouncing a Benediction". It is clear that he is not simply wishing his congregation well until next time they assemble, if that indeed has anything to do with it. But what *is* he doing? How is such a question to be decided?

Now MacIntyre's view seems to be that the intelligibility of religion depends upon a social context which has now passed away. In discussion of his paper, he suggested[13] that the

---

[13] According to N. Clarke, in his "Further Critique of MacIntyre's Thesis", where he sharpens his reply to "Is understanding religion compatible with believing?", FP 149.

meaning and relevance of the beatitudes and their opposites in the Sermon on the Mount (beginning, for example, "Blessed are you poor . . ." or "Woe to you rich . . .") are tied to a social context in which blessing and cursing are taken seriously as "social rituals". N. Clarke objects (FP 149) that MacIntyre misrepresents the beatitudes in so construing them. But, however that may be, something like a ritual of blessing, and (in some traditions) of cursing, has been retained by the Christian religion.

Some people, then, continue to take the social rituals of blessing and cursing seriously, at any rate within a religious context. Is it possible for them to do this in a society where people by and large do not take such rituals seriously? MacIntyre seems to assume that it is not. But it is difficult to see this assumption as epistemological rather than as a piece of social psychology. As a piece of social psychology it is no doubt true that there are considerable pressures which make it difficult for people to attach point to activities which are not found intelligible by society at large. But by parity of reasoning one might expect that sub-groups of a society could counteract such tendencies.

It is, for example, difficult for someone *now* to be taken seriously if he "demands satisfaction" for an insult given to himself or someone whom he respected. The social context no longer makes it possible for a man to be "honourable" in this sense. Someone who now took his own life in the face of bankruptcy in order to "save his honour" could only be regarded as sadly misguided in his conduct. We would say "misguided" because our understanding of honourable conduct would not lead us to respect such a man for acting in that way. Our social context makes such conduct look tragically quixotic. In this case, however, it is not difficult to supply the social context which would enable us to attach *some* sense to such behaviour. Historical romances, both written and enacted, have performed this imaginative project for us. Nor is it so very difficult for us to imagine an aristocratic and socially exclusive section of our own society for whom the standards of "honourable" conduct were paramount. In such a sub-group, a man would be able to preserve his self-respect and the respect of others by behaving in ways which could not intelligibly be described in the terms accepted by society as a whole as being connected with keeping one's self-respect or the respect of others.

This example seems to show that it *is* possible for a sub-group of a given society to be governed in what they do and say by standards of intelligibility not shared by society at large. It shows *this*, and not merely that there can be different codes of behaviour in a society, since the concept 'saving one's honour' does not find intelligible application except within the context of the sub-group. Nor have D-theses or C-theses provided any basis for supposing that there could not be such cases. The basis of such theses, in so far as it is epistemologically relevant is that, say, we in the United Kingdom, share a common way of life and a common way of understanding our experience. To the extent that this is not wholly true, D-theses and C-theses must go short of a satisfactory basis. They have a persuasive force, however, on account of social attitudes towards religion. It may well be true that society at large regards religion as something of a hang-over from times gone by. But it should be remembered that the study of philosophy is also viewed in this way. If it is open to the practitioners in the latter case to object that their activities have not been rightly understood, this option should equally be retained for practitioners of religion.

My criticism of MacIntyre and Bultmann has been directed not so much against the *problems* which they pose but against the way in which they try to answer them. For there *is* a problem about relating the language of religion to that of everyday life. But, whereas they have answered the problem by saying that the language of a society provides the terms in which the claims of religion can be made intelligible, I shall try to show (in Chapter X) that everyday language both gives a certain sense to religious claims and confers upon them an apparent unintelligibility. For although religious claims must be expressed in common language if people are to come to find them intelligible, simply expressing them in this way does not make such claims intelligible.

It should be said in relation to MacIntyre that those religious leaders who have welcomed the very secularization of our modes of description which makes religious belief harder are not merely being perverse. For it is arguable that such conceptual change as makes religious belief unobvious and uncompelling may not undermine faith. A society which takes such "social rituals" as blessing and cursing seriously may well turn out scrupulously on Sundays. But it may do so for reasons which are *superstitious* from the Christian point of view. It may be true that the average church-goer has little more clue as to what a minister of religion is doing when he pronounces a benediction than an unbeliever has. But it has yet to be shown that this is a modern phenomenon.

These remarks may be enlarged. There are important differences between the *social* rituals of blessing and cursing and the *Christian* rituals of blessing and cursing. The social rituals, to judge from the curious locutions that seem to have survived them ("Bless you *for that*" or "Damn you *for that*"), were responses to good or ill done to one. The Christian tradition ("Bless them that hate you") is totally opposed to such practices. So far indeed from preying on them for *its* intelligibility, it is clear from the very language that one form of cursing, namely, "damning" is parasitic on Christianity. The social ritual is here only intelligible as a perverse and superstitious[14] form of the Christian ritual of declaring someone to be "anathema", i.e. of excommunicating him. But even within those Christian traditions which provide for excommunication, great care is taken over who may perform the rite and under what conditions. History may well provide cases of retaliatory excommunication, but no churchman who admitted there to have been such cases would attempt to justify them on theological grounds.

[14] I shall discuss the nature of superstition at greater length in Chapter VII below.

The rite of pronouncing a benediction or blessing is, however, both more frequently and more widely practised amongst Christian denominations. It is variously understood but in no case is a blessing thought proper as a *quid pro quo*. It is commonly thought to be a function of the priest to pronounce a benediction, but not always the function of the priest *as opposed to the layman*, since some take the doctrine of the priesthood of all believers to be incompatible with such a separation of functions. I mention these complications because an understanding of the Christian practice of blessing cannot be gained without taking account of them.

The liturgical form of blessing seems to be decidedly "performative"[15] in character. That is to say, the priest, *in saying* certain words under certain conditions, is doing something, namely, blessing the people. One form of benediction runs as follows:[16]

"Unto God's gracious mercy and protection we commit you. And the blessing of God Almighty, the Father, the Son, and the Holy Spirit, be upon you and remain with you for ever. AMEN."

The "performative" character of this benediction seems clear from the use of the phrase "we commit you". What is the priest (or minister) *doing* in saying these words? He is committing the congregation to the mercy and protection of God. But what is it to do this? I do not pretend to know. What I have said, however, would seem to indicate that it is to the language of religion rather than that of an earlier society

[15] This term was introduced into philosophical discussion by J. L. Austin. His account was given in a set of lectures, now published in edited form by J. O. Urmson in *How to do Things with Words*, London (OUP), 1962. Obvious examples are "I name this ship *Hibernia*", "I, Charles, take you Lynette, to be my lawful wedded wife", "I second that proposal" and "I declare the meeting begun". In these cases too there are limitations on who may perform the actions done by saying these words and under what conditions. E.g. only a man can marry a woman, and only before witnesses; only the chairman can open the meeting and then only when it has been properly called.

[16] Taken from *The Book of Common Order* of the Church of Scotland, London (OUP) 1940, p. 311.

that we must look for an answer. It seems, indeed, that the answer would have to say something about what it is for a man to be a priest (or minister). It would need, that is to say, to be given in theological terms.

VI

THE QUESTION OF FACTUAL SIGNIFICANCE

A VARIETY of reasons might prompt the claim that religious utterances do not make factual claims, i.e. claims which may be considered "true" or "false". Some of these have already been considered. The phrase "devoid of factual significance" is one used by positivists in relation to religious and metaphysical pronouncements alike. For a U-thesis would—could it be sustained—license a P-thesis if it were conjoined with the thesis that the claims of religion need not be understood as "true" or "false" in character. But, if the argument of Chapter III has been sound, support for a P-thesis will need to be drawn from elsewhere.

The possibility of a P-thesis needs to be considered both from a religious and from an epistemological stand-point. On the one hand we shall need to ask whether, for example, it is possible to give an adequate account of Christianity in terms which do not represent it as involving factual claims. We shall approach this question by looking at the form of P-thesis put forward by van Buren. Van Buren is influenced by considerations which tend to favour a C-thesis or U-thesis. It would be repetitious to examine this aspect of his thought. But he is also affected on the epistemological side by arguments which afford some independent support for a P-thesis. These arguments have to do certain formal requirements to which all statement-making discourse has been thought to be subject. We must ask whether there are such requirements and whether they can be reconciled with those made on the side of religion.

17. "INSTRUMENTALISM" IN THEOLOGY

It has not been uncommon for religious apologists to advocate a view of scientific theories called "instrumentalism". According to this view, such theories are to be understood as no more than useful devices (instruments) for making predictions. This position is opposed by what is known as "realism" with regard to the status of such theories, which holds them to be such that they could properly be described as "true" or "false".

Galileo is noted for his advocacy of a realist interpretation of Copernicus' suggestion that the earth should be regarded as moving round the sun rather than vice-versa. Cardinal Bellarmine urged him to consider this only as a "supposition", as a means of predicting the movements of the heavenly bodies. As such (i.e. interpreted instrumentally) he could see "no danger" in Copernicus' suggestion. But "to wish to affirm that in reality the sun stands still in the centre of the world" is, he claimed, to adopt a position "in which there is much danger of injuring the Holy Faith by rendering false the Sacred Scriptures".[1] Bellarmine was, in effect, insisting that scientific theory should be accommodated to the Biblical cosmology by construing the former as put forward "*ex suppositione*". In any case, he pointed out, "it is not the same thing to show that the supposition that the earth moves and the sun still saves the appearances, and to demonstrate that such hypotheses are really true".[2] Galileo's arguments only showed that Copernicus' hypothesis saved the appearances. They did not show it to be "true in nature".

Van Buren's account of the "secular meaning" of Christianity might be viewed as construing the relation between science and religion in quite the opposite way. For, on his account, what can be regarded as "true" or "false" is so because empirical investigation has found it to be so. Relgious assertions

[1] *Le opere di Galileo Galilei*, Edizione Nazionale, Florence (G. Barbira) 1890, Vol. XII, p. 171f.
[2] *ibid.* Vol. V, p. 369.

cannot be regarded as "true" or "false" by this token and hence must be understood in some other way. Christian faith may provide, he thinks, new insight into the way in which human life may be understood, but not new insight into matters of fact. Affirmations of faith must not, therefore, be construed as statements of fact. Rather they are

> to be interpreted, by means of the modified verification principle, as statements which express, describe, or commend a particular way of seeing the world, other men, and oneself, and the way of life appropriate to such a perspective (SMG 156).

This account takes the use of words like "fact", "existence" and "event" as restricted in their application to what can be empirically established. Religion, as traditionally presented, involved claims about trans-empirical facts and events. But it can no longer be understood in this way. It has to be understood, rather, as providing a "historical perspective" on human life. It is *historical* in that it is based on the life and death of a historical figure, Jesus of Nazareth. It is a *perspective* in that it can affect our attitude towards life. Thus:

> The man who says, "Jesus is Lord", is saying that the history of Jesus and of what happened on Easter has exercised a liberating effect upon him, and that he has been so grasped by it that it has become the historical norm of his perspective upon life. His confession is a notification of this perspective and a recommendation to his listener to see Jesus, the world, and himself in this same way and to act accordingly (SMG 141).

The concept of 'freedom' enjoys a role central to van Buren's account which is comparable with 'authentic existence' in that given by Bultmann. Indeed van Buren describes freedom as the "logical meaning of faith". By this he does *not* mean that the words "freedom", "free" and "liberated" are actually *synonymous* with the words "faith", "faithful" and "trusting". He means rather that they provide the cash-value of this latter set of terms "in the realm of human conduct". The freedom of which he is speaking is the freedom from those anxieties which attend pre-occupation with oneself, e.g. about safety and position. On the positive side, freedom is characterized by humble service to others. The acceptance of the perspective is closely, and perhaps internally, connected to gaining this freedom. Van Buren, at any rate, does not provide for any gap between them, such that one could be present without the other.

He admits that what he is doing is reducing the Christian faith to "its historical and ethical dimensions" (SMG 200). Nevertheless he claims to have left "nothing essential" behind. He describes his account as offering "a functional equivalence between contemporary Christology and the language of the New Testament" (SMG 156). But the question remains, whether such a non-cognitive perspective can serve the same function as that served by traditional belief, whether it can sustain the same way of life as that sustained by traditional belief. We must not be required to read a "cognitive" background into such a "contemporary Christology" in order to make sense of it. For that would show that van Buren's reduction had failed.

Van Buren's discussion of traditional doctrines is interesting. But it is not free from difficulties. For example, he describes the expression "by the operation of the Holy Spirit" as indicating "that the new freedom and perspective are *received as gifts* by the believer and that they are of *fundamental importance* to him" (SMG 136, my italics). He wishes here to reflect the orthodox insistence on the passivity of the believer in relation to this "freedom". The language of faith, "by referring to a transcendent element", indicates that "something has happened to the believer, rather than that he has done something" (SMG 141). But now, does the "believer" merely *receive* this freedom *as* a gift? Or is it actually a gift? If it *is* a gift, by whom is it given? If not, why should there be any virtue in regarding it as something it is not?

At this point a secular account of Christianity has some difficulty in doing justice to its subject-matter. For the concept 'grace' can be understood *negatively* as something in no way born of any human act of will. But it could hardly be thought to be *no more* than this. So to represent it would suggest that grace just *happens* to affect some people rather than others, much as beauty spots do. But this would not only make talk of "gratitude" out of place but would also deprive the introduction of Jesus of Nazareth of any apparent relevance.

Yet what more can be added to a secular account of 'grace' which will make sense of, and therefore be a candidate for sustaining, behaviour which could be described as "grateful"? How can one add enough here without adding too much? How can one, that is to say, further specify the concept of 'grace' so as to make sense of a believer being "grateful" for his "freedom" yet stop short of making grace a gift? It seems that nothing short of a gift will make gratitude intelligible, nothing short, that is, of what is *believed to be* a gift. But once grace is squarely construed as a gift, what is believed is that there is a source of this gift, a source which will, presumably, not be empirically locatable.

It might seem that it will suffice for a "contemporary Christology" to provide room for *gladness*, that *gratitude* is not a necessary part of the Christian attitude. Thus though, for example, secularization of the concept of a 'talent' renders unintelligible such remarks as "You ought to be *grateful* to have such a fine voice", it would still make sense to say "You ought to be *glad* to have such a fine voice". But such gladness would not be enough for the Christian's attitude towards his "freedom", since such an attitude would be compatible with his regarding himself as largely responsible for it. But if this were so, pride might seem a more appropriate attitude than humility. Yet this is not the attitude which van Buren wishes to sustain by his "historical perspective". *That* attitude can only, it seems, be made intelligible within something like a traditional framework. If this is so, then his account of the secular meaning of the Gospel only makes sense when the background of traditional theology is read into it at such weak points as this. To say this, however, would be to say that such an account cannot be given.

There seems to be a more general error involved in van Buren's notion of a 'perspective'. For it cannot, at any rate as ordinarily employed, be as radically separated from the back-

ground of factual claims as he supposes. For example, when a
man is faced with the temptation to wax indignant about the
anti-social activities of someone whose circumstances have been
less fortunate than his own, he may say to himself, "There but
for the grace of God go I". It would be quite proper to
characterize what he is doing here as reminding himself of the
right perspective in which to view the anti-social behaviour of
such a man. But he can *only* do this *if* he is reminding himself
also of something he believes to be the case. This may be, in a
secular way, his belief that he himself would have behaved in
that way had his circumstances been like that. Or, taken as a
religious perspective, he may be reminding himself of what he
owes to the grace of God. In each case, the perspective's being
the right one depends entirely on whether what is believed is
true.

However, one does not say that someone is looking at some
matter "in the wrong perspective" if one believes him to be in
straightforward *error*. It is usually in matters of some complexity
where a large amount of factual information needs to be
ordered in one way or another that it becomes appropriate to
speak of "perspectives". But, though it is not easy to persuade
someone that he is looking at some matter in the wrong
perspective—think of the arguments for or against the
"domino" theory about "Communist strategy" in South-East
Asia—it is not that nothing would count as doing so. It may be
unprofitable to attempt to show that a man would be unreasonable who refused to accept the Christian religion. Van Buren
may be right, in this sense, in regarding natural theology as a
"dead end". But this does not mean that Christian "insights"
cannot be regarded as true, that they cannot be thought to
provide a "true perspective". It is not clear what could be
meant by speaking of a "perspective" at all if such a possibility
does not remain open.

Van Buren himself does not succeed in avoiding the use of
cognitive expressions, e.g. he speaks of the presentation of the
Gospel as "an invitation to the listener to share this *discernment*"
(SMG 152f., italics mine). But he is usually cautious enough to

surround such expressions with inverted commas. For example, he says that, as long as a man holds on to a given perspective, "the world he sees through it is for him the world as it 'really' is'" (SMG 161). But this use of inverted commas is puzzling. It looks very much as if van Buren is here doing no more than merely *mentioning* the phrase which the (philosophically unreflective) believer would employ rather than *using* the word "really" himself. The suggestion seems to be that this is how it would appear to be to such a believer, though "of course" it is not actually like that. And this makes van Buren's position even more like that of the instrumentalist. For the instrumentalist will want to say that the practising scientist who speaks of theories as "true" is, in a way, quite right, only he has put matters infelicitously. And in just the same way, van Buren seems to be saying that the practising believer who speaks, e.g. of the "facts" of redemption is, in a sense, quite right. Only this, it might be said, is an unsophisticated way of putting it, one which is not informed by the difficulties which beset taking such locutions strictly and seriously.

If, however, van Buren is thus far committed to a religious counterpart of what is called "instrumentalism" with regard to scientific theories, it may seem open to him to make the riposte against "realist" criticism which is commonly made by instrumentalists. It is to maintain that, contrary to appearances, the issue between them is a *purely verbal* one. It is, that is to say, an issue over the terms which we are to choose in speaking of religious utterances. It seems, indeed, that van Buren is already at least half-inclined to such a view, since his account suggests that it does not matter too much how we speak so long as a "functional equivalence" is preserved. The consideration which makes the terms of his "contemporary Christology" preferable have to do with the firmly empirical character of contemporary attitudes. From the point of view of the Christian faith as such, it might be said to make no difference whether it is expressed in one way or another.

It is, however, necessary to an instrumentalist account that its language should make sense in its own right and not require to presuppose what can only be accounted for in realist terms. This has been one large bone of contention with regard to the issue of realism over against instrumentalism (more commonly known as "phenomenalism") about material objects. In this case the instrumentalists have been inclined to maintain that material objects are no more than pragmatic figments. The assumption of such objects is of some value to us in co-ordinating our sense-contents and in enabling us to make reliable predictions regarding the nature of our future sense-contents. But, it is claimed, such an assumption is not needed for the stricter purposes of a philosophical account. Yet it would be needed if it were only possible to make sense of the language of sense-contents by re-introducing the notion of a 'material object'. If such a lack of self-sufficiency could be established against a phenomenalist language, this would constitute as strong an argument for realism as could be desired.

It seems possible to defend theological realism against van Buren's analogue of instrumentalism on just this score. For in order to make sense of his "contemporary Christology" we need to re-introduce the traditional language of religion. To this extent realism seems to be a requirement on the side of religion. For if grace must be thought of as a gift some reference is needed to its source. Yet it does not seem possible to speak of the source of this gift without speaking of "truths" which cannot be rendered intelligible in wholly secular terms.

Nevertheless it may be that it must be insisted, on the side of epistemology, that the claims of religion do not qualify as "true" or "false" in character. This would be tantamount to showing that such claims do not live up to their pretensions.

18. UNFALSIFIABLE CLAIMS

It is a feature of certain central religious claims, of statements of faith in particular, that their advocates show no inclination to count anything as tending to *falsify* them. They do not, indeed, claim that their beliefs could be established so as to become items of knowledge. In such matters, they say, we see "as in a glass, darkly". Faith is a religious virtue. On the religious side, it is regarded as praiseworthy for a man to persist in his belief in a loving God, the more so if the circumstances in which he finds himself make such a belief difficult.

Just these considerations, however, have been thought to make religious belief suspect, from an epistemological point of view. For how can a belief that something is the case be so immune from the risk of falsification? Surely, it is urged, religious assertions can only enjoy their fact-proof character at a price, namely, the price of emptiness, of not saying anything about what is the case.

R. M. Hare,[3] for example, was led into a form of P-thesis by just this consideration, that nothing would be counted by those who put forward such claims as telling against them. The difference between the believer and the unbeliever is, on his account, to be described as that between people who have different "bliks". He explains what he means by a "blik" in the following way:

> Suppose we believed that everything that happened, happened by pure chance. This would not of course be an assertion; for it is compatible with anything happening or not happening, and so, incidentally, is its contradictory. But if we had this belief, we should not be able to explain or predict or plan anything. Thus, although we would not be *asserting* anything different from those of a more normal belief, there would be a great difference between us. . . .

Hare's point is that it is a mark of a proper assertion that something should count against its being true, whereas it is a mark of a "blik" that its adherent may hold on to it come what may. Hare's account has the novelty that it allows someone to believe something without *believing it to be true*, though he does not indicate how we could speak of "belief" in this way. Nor does he attempt to justify the view that a proper assertion must be such that something would count against its being true. His use of the phrase "of course", however, indicates—

[3] *New Essays in Philosophical Theology*, London (SCM Press) ed. Flew & MacIntyre and New York (Macmillan) 1955, p. 101 f.

what is in fact the case—that such a view has acquired the status of an orthodoxy.

Some argument for such an orthodoxy is to be found in G. J. Warnock's article entitled "Every event has a cause".[4] Hare seems to speak as if this utterance were a genuine assertion. For he says that its "contradictory" is "everything that happens, happens by pure chance". But to speak in this way is to suggest precisely what Hare wishes to deny, namely, that it is a *genuine* assertion. For only what has truth-value can be or have a contradictory. Warnock uses language which equally seems to suggest just what he is overtly denying. For he speaks as if "every event has a cause" was an *assertion*, only one which is *vacuous*. But a vacuous assertion would be one which *said* nothing and by that token it would not really be an assertion at all. Thus Warnock, like Hare, wishes to claim that "every event has a cause" is not a genuine assertion on the ground that it is "compatible" with whatever takes place. But this is, on the face of it, a curious reason for claiming that an apparent assertion is not really an assertion. For only an assertion— only what *has* truth-value—could be compatible or incompatible with its being the case that some state of affairs obtains. The criticism thus seems to be self-refuting.

It would, however, be wrong to take such a short way with this view. For it may be said in defence of it that it is only by treating a putative assertion as though it were a genuine assertion that its bogus character can be exposed. There cannot, it may be said, be genuine assertions (other than tautologies) which a man may continue to make no matter what happens. In treating something as an assertion we expect to find that some state of affairs would, if it obtained, count as grounds for refusing to make it. If that expectation is disappointed, we will have to say that we were mistaken in so treating it. Or so it might be said.

Let us, then, look more closely at Warnock's argument. For the sake of precision he considers a more definite formulation

[4] *Logic and Language*, Series II, ed. Antony Flew, Oxford (Blackwell) 1953, Ch. VI.

of "every event has a cause". This, which he calls "S" for short, runs as follows:

"For any event E, there is some set of antecedent conditions such that, whenever these conditions obtain, an event of the kind E occurs." In considering the status of S, he argues that "there could never occur an event which it would be necessary, or even natural, to describe as an uncaused event". This makes S look like some kind of necessary truth, since "it is completely independent of the actual course of events, compatible with anything and everything which may happen". In this respect it is like "The Bishop is to be moved diagonally". However, unlike such a rule of a game, it *seems* to say something about the actual course of events. Yet if it has this independence from the actual course of events when it comes to asking whether or not it is true, it cannot, in Warnock's opinion, be held to be *about* the actual course of events. It looks rather, since we may assert it "without fear of mistake", that it must be necessary in some way without being true of the actual course of events.

But, Warnock goes on to say:

> This is not to say, what I think is plainly untrue, that S is tautologous or analytic. It resembles a tautology in being compatible with any and every state of affairs; but it escapes the possibility of falsification not because it is necessary, but rather because it is vacuous. It is more like the assertion that there are invisible, intangible, odorless, soundless, and otherwise indetectable tigers in the garden—though it is less conspicuously vacuous than this, the reasons for its unfalsifiability being different and much less obvious (op. cit., p. 107).

Warnock does not, unfortunately, provide any further clarification of the vacuous character of S. But his suggestion seems to be that if we examined the tiger-example carefully, we should uncover considerations which betray the less obvious vacuity of S. One way of approaching the tiger example is to see it as a case of a claim which has been made as a result of qualifications which have been made to avoid being found to have been in error. If someone claims that there is a tiger in the garden, it may, unless the garden is exceptionally large, be readily ascertained whether or not what he says is true. If, on examination, no tiger is found, it might (by someone reluctant to be shown wrong) be claimed that we have only *looked*. The tiger, he may say, is invisible, so it is small wonder that we cannot find it just by looking. So microphones are placed at suitable points around the garden, but still with no result. It is a soundless, invisible tiger, we are told. This is still intelligible, for we can imagine finding someone who claimed to have been attacked by the tiger and who bore the marks of mauling which experts assure us are characteristic. But no one is attacked. An intangible tiger, we are told. By now the claim being advanced is so qualified as to suffer what Flew has termed "the death by a thousand qualifications".[5] It has been so qualified that the claim has become quite vacuous, i.e. ceased to be a claim at all.

The reason, however, why such a claim, so modified, becomes vacuous seems to have to do with the character of the concept 'tiger' which we have. It is an empirical concept and, as such, is governed in its application by observational criteria. The idea of a 'non-observable tiger' is one which does not make sense to us. Hence it is natural to take the claim about there being a tiger in the garden as empirical in character. Yet it is so modified as to make no sense as an empirical claim at all. For it is a condition of an empirical claim being such that it should be amenable to falsification, in particular that it should be controvertible by experience.

The case with S, however, does not seem to be the same. For whereas our man who over-qualifies his claim that there is a tiger in the garden ends up by not being able to say what would count against his claim, advocates of S are not similarly placed. For they could say that, in claiming S, they are excluding the case where it could be established with regard to a given event E that it had taken place in the absence of those conditions under which alone events of that kind can take place. It would not be enough, of course, to establish that E

[5] *New Essays in Philosophical Theology*, p. 97. Just this line of argument against the intelligibility of religious claims is advanced by Flew by means of his well-known version of the "Invisible Gardener" argument.

had occurred without the prior holding of those conditions under which alone it was *thought* an event of that kind could occur. For that would present no problem, save of re-thinking what the true causes of E-like events might be. It would be necessary to establish *both* that it was quite impossible for E-like events to occur except under certain conditions *and* that nevertheless E did quite certainly occur when those conditions had not obtained. A man might subscribe to S in the belief that either these claims *could* not ever be jointly established or that in no case *would* they ever be jointly established.

I shall return to this question shortly. But some observations are now in place about the status of S. For it is of considerable importance in assessing its status that two requirements be distinguished: (1) that the making of a genuine claim or assertion must commit a man to denying some other claim; and (2) that for a claim to be factual (i.e. to be true or false) in character, there must be considerations which would count against it. Now it is true that the tiger case fails to satisfy (2). But this, it might be said, only counts against it as a claim to be true *as a matter of fact*. In this case, admittedly, there seems no other way of construing the claim except as one putatively stating a matter of fact. The reason why such a claim, through excessive modification, becomes unintelligible is that, given the concept 'tiger' which we have, it is not clear that anyone who makes it is thereby committed to denying anything, except of course its formal contradictory. This is not so, by contrast, with S. For someone who subscribed to it might, in so doing, be committed to denying that there could be, or would be, super- natural intervention in the course of events. And if it could be shown to amount to more than a subtly disguised denial of S's formal contradictory that he would be committed to, then his advocacy of S meets requirement (1).

Requirement (1) is indeed a quite general condition of intelligible (statement-making) discourse. For suppose, to take an example, someone is prepared to say of *everything whatever* that it is "schmarsh". I do not mean someone who would say this in the way in which someone might say that everything whatever is "imperfect", for we might, given some explanation, understand such a claim. I mean someone who is prepared to assert, not only of all *actual* items he encounters, but of all *possible* items he might encounter, that they are "schmarsh". We could not, it is clear, ever discover what he meant by the word "schmarsh". But more than this, we could not—if there is nothing he would *count as* an item being other than "schmarsh" —allow that *he* could mean anything by the "word". We could, with confidence, dismiss his utterances as pseudo-claims. For no statement, under these conditions, could be made by them.

Once, however, we are able to detect circumstances in which such a man will refuse to call something "schmarsh", we may be able to extrapolate a rule which will give us some idea of what he means by the word. For example, we might find that he does not call things he regards as beautiful "schmarsh". We may thus provisionally suppose that what he means by it is something like "ugly". And of course it may be that the meaning of the word can be still further specified, by a closer examination of his use of the word. It may turn out, for instance, to be a special kind of aesthetic deficiency he senses in some works of art for which he has coined this term for want of another already available to him from the stock of words he possesses.

Now this *formal* requirement might be said to be met by, for example, the claim that everything that happens, happens according to the will of God. This belief is, of course, compatible with the thesis that men *do* what is not according to the will of God. For men's actions are not, in the sense intended, "happenings". The view is, that God is omnipotent and therefore that anything which happens must be in accordance with his will. A man who accepted it would be committed to denying the existence of rival supernatural powers who, over some matters, could cause events to happen contrary to the will of God. But, whatever may be wrong about such a belief, it is not "vacuous" in the sense in which "Everything is 'schmarsh' " is vacuous. For whereas all that someone who made the latter claim would be committed to denying is that there is not anything that is not "schmarsh", the commitments of someone who holds that everything which happens, happens in accordance with the will of God are not nearly so tenuous. For though such a claim does fail to satisfy requirement (2), it meets requirement (1), since anyone who made it would presumably be committed to a particular view of evil. Natural disasters would have to be viewed as in some sense not "evil" from such a religious standpoint, namely, in that sense in which something is "evil" if, and only if, it is contrary to the will of God. To suppose that such disasters were in this sense "evil" would be incompatible with the belief in question. But such a supposition is by no means a bare formal contradictory of what is affirmed in such a belief.

The manner in which Warnock, Hare and Flew present[6] the issue of factual significance glosses over the distinction between these two requirements. The logical bite of the first requirement is thus transferred to the second, more problematic, requirement. Such a transference would only be justifiable if it could be insisted that all statements which can be said to be "true" are either so as a matter of fact or because of conventions governing our symbolism. I have, in criticizing the conventionalist position in Chapter IV, already questioned one side of the received distinction between "analytic" and "contingent" truths. In doing so, I have suggested that there are claims to which a certain necessity attaches since it would make no sense to deny them. I have called these "grammatical claims" as opposed to what might be called "matter-of-fact" claims. This distinction may now be examined in relation to requirement (2). How, that is to say, are *matter-of-fact* and *grammatical* claims respectively affected by the requirement

---

[6] Warnock does this by objecting to S on the ground that it is "compatible with any and every state of affairs", whereas Hare says that something would fail to be an assertion if it were "compatible with anything happening or not happening". Flew (*New Essays*, p. 98f.) writes as if the second requirement were equivalent to the first. For though he concludes (rightly) that "if there is nothing which a putative assertion denies then there is nothing which it asserts either", he assumes that what must be denied is that what would be counted as telling against the assertion in question actually obtains.

that, for a claim to be factually significant, it must be such that something would count against its being true?

There are, it has been noted, two distinct positions which might be adopted in claiming that every event has a (natural) cause. One of these positions involves construing this claim as a *matter-of-fact* generalization. So construed, it does meet requirement (2). For in allowing sense to the phrase "lacking a (natural) cause" it provides for circumstances in which it might be falsified. The claim, so construed, is that we will never in fact have occasion correctly to describe an event as lacking a natural cause.

It is the second position which might be adopted which falls foul of requirement (2). In this respect an espousal of the claim "Every event has a cause" is analogous, so understood, to an affirmation of faith. They may indeed share the same fate or fortune in relation to this requirement. Certainly it would be wrong to suppose that the claims of religion must be regarded as wholly anomalous, from an epistemological stand-point. The case for supposing that the requirement does not vitiate the pretension of religion to contain claims as to what is the case must depend on the claims of religion being shown to have a status which exempts them from this requirement. If, then, affirmations of faith can be shown to share with this second position the character of being "grammatical": and if, further, it can be shown that requirement (2) does not need to be met by grammatical claims, it may be possible to transfer the results of such a finding to affirmations of faith.

I have said that "grammatical" claims may be thought of as in a sense "necessarily" true. To accept a claim as true in this way is to accept it as one which could not *conceivably* be false. I have also indicated that this kind of claim is not "analytic" in character. It may seem, therefore, that I am undertaking to defend *synthetic a priori* truth. But this is not so. For in the first place I do not wish to accept the rigid structure of relations between concepts which is implied by that sense of "analytic" normally contrasted with what is "synthetic". In the second place I have not wished to say that grammatical claims could be *known* to be true, still less that they could be known to be true quite apart from any experience. Both the terms "synthetic" and "*a priori*" are therefore out of place.

It is a feature of grammatical claims that they may appear more readily as what someone is *committed* to by virtue of other claims than as what he explicitly *avows*. Hume, for example, would have found it quite inconsistent with his philosophical tenets to treat the causal principle as any kind of necessary truth. Yet there is some reason to believe that even he allowed himself to be committed to it by virtue of his treatment of miracles. In his essay on the subject, he speaks mostly as if the issue were one of probabilities. His conclusion *seems* to be that, although "violations of laws of nature" are possible, they are sufficiently improbable for it to be reasonable to suppose that there never has been any case of one in all history. Hume cites a case which would, it seems, have counted as a miracle, had it occurred. But his treatment of it suggests that he is not really prepared to admit even this case as a *bona fide* violation of the laws of nature. He seems indeed to rule out any possibility of anything being counted as such a violation. To that extent it seems to become a matter of grammar, on the view Hume takes, that violations of laws of nature cannot occur.

One of the main lines of argument against the likelihood of a miracle ever having occurred is that the evidence against such a contingency is *initially* so great that testimony of witnesses could scarcely hope to establish one. For, since a miracle is a violation of a *law of nature*, all the weight of human experience which tells in favour of counting the law as such must be added to the balance over against the testimony of the witnesses. The probability of the witnesses being mistaken or prejudiced is, in all cases which history may provide us with, always likely to be greater than the probability of the event's having actually happened. The argument, so presented, is one concerning probabilities. We are always to "reject the greater miracle" or, in other words, believe what is more probable.

Hume does not, that is to say, officially rule out the possibility of such violations of laws of nature. He even gives an example of what would count as such a "violation":

> ... suppose all authors, in all languages, agree that, from the 1st of January, 1600, there was a total darkness over the whole earth for eight days: suppose that the tradition of this extraordinary event is still strong and lively among the people: suppose that all travellers who return from foreign countries bring us accounts of the same tradition, without the least variation or contradiction: it is evident that our present philosophers ought to receive it as certain. . . . (EHU 127f.)

This, had it been all that Hume wrote about this case, would have confirmed the view which he seemed earlier concerned to advance, namely, that the issue was one about probabilities. On such a view, "violations" of laws of natures could not be ruled out in principle. *But* this is not all that Hume says. For he finishes his sentence by saying that "our present philosophers ought to receive it as certain *and ought to search for the causes whence it might be derived*". But the addition of the words I have italicized alters the picture completely. For if Hume had actually been prepared to count this case as genuinely a miracle, he could not consistently have said that its possible causes ought to be explored. For the attempt to find a natural cause of the event would, for someone who had made such a concession, have no point. In commending such an attempt to discover the causes he is, in fact, refusing to make the concession he appears to have made. And, in refusing to make it, he is ruling out the possibility of there being such a miracle. In so doing, he seems to commit himself to a thesis— quite contrary to Humean principles—that all events do have natural causes and that nothing would count as an event which was an exception to this rule.

One might describe Hume's attitude towards miracles as treating the issue regarding them officially as a *matter-of-fact* one but unofficially as a *grammatical* one. In so far as the former view of them is the one we would be most justified in ascribing to Hume, his account meets requirement (2). But, in so far as he is committed to excluding the possibility of miracles occurring by refusing to admit the terms on which such a possibility can be countenanced, he is committed to a thesis which conflicts with this requirement. This is of some historical interest, in that Hume may be credited with doing much to pioneer that distinction between truths which depend on the comparison of ideas and those which depend on matters of fact which I am calling in question by introducing the concept of a 'grammatical claim'.

R. F. Holland[7] has put forward an account of the "violation" concept of miracle which would, if it were correct, undermine the thesis that nothing would count as an event lacking in a natural cause. For he argues that it is possible to imagine the occurrence of events which are both "empirically certain" and "conceptually impossible", events which therefore involve a "conflict of certainties". It would need to involve something as strong as a conflict of certainties, for the following reason:

> If it were less than conceptually impossible it would reduce merely to a very unusual occurrence such as could be treated (because of the empirical certainty) in the manner of a decisive experiment and result in a modification to the prevailing conception of natural law; while if it were less than empirically certain nothing more would be called for in regard to it than a suspension of judgment (RU 167).

Holland offers three examples of what it would be appropriate to describe as "miracles" in this sense. He notes the common objection that "while there is such a thing as not knowing what the cause or explanation of a phenomenon might be there can be no such thing as establishing the absence of a cause" (RU 168). Hence it might always seem possible to cling on to the view that a natural explanation must be available whatever happens. (And such a view would violate the second requirement.) But Holland considers his example of the New

[7] In an article entitled "The miraculous" (*American Philosophical Quarterly*, Vol. II, 1965), reprinted in RU 155ff.

Testament story of the turning of water into wine as counting decisively against such a view. He describes this example in the following terms:

> At one moment, let us suppose, there was water and at another moment wine, in the same vessel, although nobody had emptied out the water and poured in the wine. This is something which could conceivably have been established with certainty. What is not conceivable is that it could have been done by a device. Nor is it conceivable that there could have been a natural cause of it. For this would have had to be the natural cause of the water's becoming wine. And water's becoming wine is not the description of any conceivable natural process. It is conceptually impossible that the wine could have been got naturally from water. . . . (RU 168)

This argument makes considerable use of expressions like "inconceivable" and "conceptually impossible". It seems what Holland intends in saying of something that it is "conceptually impossible" is that it would *make no sense*. There is, he wishes to say, more than one kind of conceptual impossibility. Cases of *self*-contradiction (RU 167) are one kind, but not the kind on which he is here focussing his attention. For there are cases of contradiction which arise curiously out of the fact that what is described is in some way a contradiction in one's experience. He thinks this is so in the case of St John's "description" of the water-into-wine episode (RU 169). In a sense nothing is effectively described by what St John offers. But one might say that "something has been . . . garbled". For it is not just what is *said* which is difficult. There is also "such a thing as making sense, and failing to make sense, of *events*" (RU 170). John's "description" is infected by the unintelligibility of the state of affairs he purports to describe. That it makes no sense to *claim* that someone has turned water into wine is due to the fact that we are unable to make sense of someone's *doing* this.

Holland holds it to be conceivable that the conceptually impossible (or *in*conceivable) might occur. But this, it might seem, is a curious position to adopt. For, it might be thought, *if* a given event's occurring is *in*conceivable, then it is *not* conceivable that it should occur. How then could it be said of that event that it could conceivably occur? *Only*, it would seem, if the sense in which it is "conceivable" that it should occur is a different sense from that opposed in saying of it that it is "inconceivable" that it should occur. The first sense must, moreover, be weaker and its opposed sense of "inconceivable" correspondingly stronger, if this is to be admissable. Some notion of 'logical possibility' would be weak enough, and the corresponding notion of 'logical impossibility' strong enough, for this purpose. It may well be that it is some such notion that Holland has in mind. For when he introduces the water-into-wine story he makes it clear that he is concerned to argue, not that the story actually is, but that it "logically could be" true. This being so, his notion of a 'conceptual impossibility' must be weaker than that notion of 'logical impossibility' which applies to cases of *self*-contradiction. Holland seems to want to say that a statement can be contradictory but not *self*-contradictory. He thinks, at any rate, that there is a very strong sense of "*in*conceivable" (which is yet weaker than "logically im-possible") which would enable us to rule out the possibility of certain descriptions of events being true with certainty.

The question is, whether there is available to Holland a sense of "conceptually impossible" which could serve this purpose. If there were, it would be possible to refute a man who wished to say that a natural cause of the occurrence in question might yet be found. His belief could thus be denied a "grammatically necessary" status in so far as it could be shown that it could not escape the risk of falsification. Holland seems to think his water-into-wine example decisively refutes the man who thinks we may continue to hope for a natural explanation of any event. But it is difficult to see on what norms of intelligibility we may rely in deriving the inconceivability of this case if not those implicit in the language of science. And if, given the radical changes which are possible in scientific theory, those norms may themselves change, there is a loophole here for the person who is reluctant to accept *any* event as counting as one "lacking a natural cause".

Holland himself wishes to rely more on what he calls "common understanding" than appeals to scientific theory. For he writes:

> ... that water could conceivably have been turned into wine in the first century A.D. by means of a device is ruled out of court by common understanding; and though the verdict is supported by scientific knowledge, common understanding has no need of this support (RU 168).

But his reliance on "common understanding" does not commit him to viewing it as dependable *in the face of* scientific findings to the contrary. Yet, without adopting such a standpoint, he cannot close the "loop-hole" provided by the possibility of radical changes in scientific theory.

His examples are, therefore, *less than* "decisive". They do, however, put sufficient pressure on the view that every event has a natural cause to make such a view appear more like an "article of faith" than, say, a "presupposition of scientific inquiry". For while there is this loop-hole, the case for not availing oneself of it may be made as plausible as the case for taking advantage of it. It might not be too fanciful a hope that some change or development of scientific theory might render intelligible such "phenomena" as those much-canvassed cases of "telepathy". But there may be areas in which it would be excessively pious to hope for a suitably drastic change. And the examples Holland cites[8] may well fall in these areas. It may be that if such phenomena could be established as having occurred, it would be as reasonable to regard them as wholly anomalous and lacking in a natural explanation as it would be to persist in the search for such an explanation of them. Even if such a situation has never in fact arisen, it cannot be ruled out as a matter of logic. In that sense it is conceivable that the inconceivable might occur.

If we admitted this, however, it could have a disturbing effect on our confidence in our conception of reality. It is

---

[8] He gives two other examples: one is of a horse maintaining itself in good health over a long period of time without any form of nutrition, the other is of a man maintaining himself in mid-air without any means of support or device for preventing his falling.

perhaps in defence of that conception of reality that we may wish to insist on taking advantage of the loop-hole, for all that it appears as a matter of faith for us to do so. This situation is one of a grammatical claim under duress. Were it abandoned, new concepts would be needed to provide the terms in which we could attempt to understand such contingencies. We should then be trying to make it "conceivable" in a stronger sense that the scientifically inconceivable should occur. But we should only *have* to do this if the occasion demanded it. As things stand, we could maintain that a natural cause can, *as a matter of fact*, be found for any phenomenon. And Holland, though this is not one of the express purposes of his article, has provided us with a means of doing so.

One objection which might be raised against describing the claim that every event has a cause as "grammatical" in character is that it does not obviously fit into the type of case described in Chapter IV. It is indeed difficult for a twentieth-century European to regard such a claim as providing him with any kind of "insight". On the contrary, he may be inspired by recent developments in physical theory, in particular by the Principle of Uncertainty, to suppose that a new concept of scientific explanation[9] is required from that implied in such a view. For, whereas the claim that every event has a cause represents scientific explanation as *causal* in character, it might be thought that some insight was involved in seeing that it could be represented as *statistical*. Talk about a causal principle may seem to provide a context in relation to which a different view of scientific explanation might appear insightful. It does not seem to be itself such as to enlarge our understanding.

To this objection it may be replied that the kind of grammatical claim which is being characterized as more than conventionally true is so because *some* context can be provided

[9] A sophisticated presentation of this different way of seeing scientific explanation is to be found in R. B. Braithwaite's book *Scientific Explanation*, Cambridge University Press 1953, Harper Torchbook edition 1960. He suggests that "it will be safer for the philosopher to take statistical hypotheses as being the normalcy" in view of the "irreducibly statistical form of explanation" (p. 116) adopted in quantum mechanics.

in relation to which it may be seen, by those who hold it to be thus more than conventionally true, as expressing an "insight". *Our* understanding is not helped by the grammatical claim that every event has a natural cause. But someone whose life had been dominated by the fear of supernatural forces acting against him might view this claim very differently, could he be brought to accept it. It is likely that we should have to introduce such a man to our concept of a 'natural cause'. If that were so, his description of the forces he feared as "supernatural" would be retrospective.

The difficulties, however, which have inclined philosophers to deny the factual significance of religious assertions on account of their failure to meet requirement (2) are not solved by distinguishing between grammatical and matter-of-fact claims. On the contrary, they are accentuated and seen to have a wider bearing. Indeed, in introducing a notion of a 'grammatical claim' which avoids the difficulties of a conventionalist position, the argument runs headlong into a dilemma which the conventionalist will not be slow to spot. For, it may be argued, any claim that something is the case *must*, since the notion of 'truth' is introduced, involve some *pretension to objectivity*. But a dilemma arises when the attempt is made to present grammatical claims as though they could live up to such a pretension. For either it is possible to decide on rational grounds between competing grammatical claims or it is not. If it is possible, then it can only be possible if requirement (2) is met, i.e. if something will count as tending to falsify such claims. But *this* would in turn be possible only if such claims were *other* than grammatical in character, which *ex hypothesi* they are not. Yet, if it is not possible to decide between competing grammatical claims on rational grounds, the objectivity requirement is not met. If it is not met, then such claims cannot be regarded as strictly "true" or "false". This consequence would lead us directly back to a conventionalist position.

This dilemma might be put crudely by saying that so-called "grammatical claims" can either be grammatical or be claims, but *not both*. It is one which, for reasons which should become apparent, must be faced by anyone who is contemplating any form of B-thesis. Some preliminary discussion may now be given to the questions it poses and to the kinds of answer which may be given to them.

20. THE PROBLEM OF OBJECTIVITY

One way of coping with this dilemma is to deny the pretension to objectivity said to be involved in the claim that something is "true" or "false". And since there is a temptation to suppose that *any* form of B-thesis *must* be committed[10] to just such a denial, it will be appropriate to begin by considering one advocate of a B-thesis who makes such a denial quite explicitly. He is W. F. Zuurdeeg, who roundly declares that "'the problem of objectivity' does not exist" (APR 47).

Zuurdeeg tries to keep normative epistemology at bay through his emphatic denial that it is the philosopher's job to "decide whether the reality meant in a certain language is 'really' there or not" (APR 45). The philosopher can do no more than "to notice that if human beings speak either indicative or convictional language they refer to something which is 'real' for them". Zuurdeeg's distinction between "indicative" and "convictional" language is in some respects analogous to that drawn here between "matter-of-fact" and "grammatical" claims. It is, for example, a mark of "indicative" as opposed to "convictional" language that claims made in it are verifiable (APR 35). "Convictional" language has its use in matters of general interpretation, e.g. "the meaning of history". All sciences are "built upon some specific assumptions of a convictional character". One such "assumption" is that "'reality' is rational, at least to such an extent that there is a possibility for human beings to gain a reliable picture of it, if they approach it with their intellect" (APR 49).

[10] MacIntyre, for example, seems to suppose just this, to judge from the confidence with which he ascribes a position of "total relativism" (FP 120) to Winch. I do not know in what terms Winch would wish to avoid such a position, but he does not espouse it and it would require a good deal more argument than MacIntyre gives to show that he cannot avoid it.

The similarity between "convictional" language and "grammatical" claims does not, however, extend very far in detail. Each is indeed characteristic of, but not peculiar to, religion. Zuurdeeg applies his arguments to ideologies (APR 35ff.), which are here neglected. More controversially, he applies them to the sciences. It will be apparent that the "grammatical" claims of science form an area of inquiry which, through neglect of conceptual change, has remained largely unexplored by philosophers of science. I have suggested, in Section 8 above, that the Principle of Uncertainty (at any rate as presented by Dingle) is "grammatical". The problem of objectivity might be expressed with regard to this principle by asking whether, given that no crucial experiment could falsify it, it can properly be described as "true"?

Zuurdeeg expresses this problem in a more general way by asking whether, if "indicative" language cannot be freed (as he maintains it cannot) from "convictional" elements, the objectivity of science is not thereby threatened. It is in this context that he sets about laying the ghost of a view of science as totally objective, in the sense of being free from all presuppositions. In doing this, he commits himself to a relativist view of truth. He does not, of course, mean by this that we can say what we please. Truth is not, for him, "a matter of fancy or imagination". But nor can it be defined as "*quod ubique, semper, et ab omnibus creditum est*". For no discourse can be free from "convictional" elements. Hence he says:

> No product of scientific investigation may be called objective, because the subjective element can never be completely expelled. However, it is not necessary for a theory to remain purely subjective. At the end of the process of scientific research and criticism, it can be raised to the intersubjective level (APR 291).

This way of handling the problem of objectivity might be said to involve *reducing* the notion of 'objectivity' to that of 'intersubjectivity'. It takes on, indeed, a sociological aspect:

> Truth is relative. There is no absolute truth. What is generally accepted as the most plausible explanation of a group of facts, is relative to the century in which we live, and to the personal

characteristics and background of the scholars who set forth the theory (APR 290).

Zuurdeeg's account might be expressed in the following way: A statement may be said to be "true" at a given time if it is agreed, subject to the accepted processes of criticism and discussion, to be such by "the majority of recognized scholars". Theological truth is no more ultimate than scientific truth. "People revise their theological language, however, not on the basis of new facts and theories, but by the force of new insights, in the sense of deepened convictions" (APR 292). What may be true *for us* may not have been true for our ancestors and may not be true for generations to come. Strictly speaking, we should always qualify our claim that something is true with the phrase "for us". Intersubjectivity prevents what I claim being true merely for myself, but it would be a mistake to suppose it could make my claims true *without qualification*.

It is of some significance that Zuurdeeg rarely mentions "truth", "knowledge" or "reality" except in inverted commas. For he tends to assimilate the question: "*What* do people claim when they claim to know something to be true?" to the question: "*When* do people claim to know that something is true?" It may very well be the case that a scientist, for example, will only say that "we now know that" such-and-such is the case *when* the majority of those researching in the relevant field would agree with him. But it does not follow from this that *what* he would be claiming in introducing the word "know" in such a context is just that he can count on such agreement. Similarly, in supporting the truth of his claim, he will no doubt indicate what makes him and his fellow-researchers hold it to be true. But he is not merely saying what makes *them* accept it. He is also *justifying* the claim he has advanced. It may well be that the terms of his justification will reflect the outlook and theory shared by a particular generation of workers in his field. But, in claiming that something is true, he is not claiming that it is "*true for*" that particular generation of scientists of which he is a member. He is, on the contrary, simply claiming it to be true.

There is, in other words, some pretension to objectivity beyond that which can be indicated in the notion of 'inter-subjectivity' involved in the claim that something is "true". This holds also of any belief that something is "true". It may be for this reason that claims and beliefs, whilst they may be rational or irrational, cannot be a-rational. Zuurdeeg seems to have made the mistake of supposing that, since I must, in justifying a belief, give the reasons which make me accept it, the nature of those reasons must restrict what is being claimed. For what will be acceptable as good reasons in one community may well not be acceptable in another. Hence, he supposes, what is claimed to be true for those reasons can only be true for the community which accepts them. But the beliefs of one group or generation are not that immune from criticism by another. It used to be believed in medieval England that weasels gave birth to their young through their ears. But we are under no compunction to say that this belief was true relative to anything—though of course it was *thought* to be true. That belief, if I have represented it correctly, is false.

Matters are, however, much more complex when the issues are *grammatical* rather than *matter-of-fact*. For they are not decidable by reference to mutually-agreed considerations. I have mentioned some cases of this kind of disagreement in Chapter IV. In Section 12, for example, two different concepts of 'hypocrisy' and 'sincerity' were discussed. On one account, it was held that a hypocrite *must* regard himself as insincere. On the other account, it was held that he *may* regard himself as sincere. Now it is clear that those who hold these different concepts of hypocrisy will not agree in all their judgments regarding particular cases. For, in accordance with their differing grammatical claims, they will not agree as to what is to be counted as a "hypocrite" or, for that matter, a case of "insincerity". Hence, viewed as factual disputes, their disagreements over particular cases will seem to involve their talking at cross-purposes.

It is tempting to say in such a case that the issue between them is "merely verbal", that it is the result of their adopting different conventions regarding the use of the word "hypo-crite". This would be so, however, only if both parties *under-stood* the cases in the same way. In that event they might still choose to describe them with different terms. Then one party may say that those supposed cases of "hypocrisy" involving self-deception are not cases of what he would choose to call "hypocrisy" at all.

But this is not the case as described. For it was an important feature of the case described that a different understanding of hypocrisy is involved. It is by virtue of this different under-standing that licence may be given to speak of "insight" in respect of one party to the dispute. For that party claims to recognize as *true* what the other party is committed to dis-missing as unintelligible, namely, that the hypocrite may regard himself as sincere. But, in claiming so to recognize the truth of the claim that the hypocrite *may* regard himself as sincere, one would be committed to denying the truth of the claim that the hypocrite *must* regard himself as *in*sincere. The issue is not merely a verbal one. It is one, rather, about the terms in which certain forms of human behaviour may best be understood.

The error which seems to lie at the root of conventionalism is that the terms in which we describe the world can be radically divorced from our understanding of it. It is of course true that the actual symbolism we use is arbitrary and conventional. If this were not so, we could never translate anything from one language into another. But the concepts which we have— and therefore in one sense the "terms" which we are able to employ—are not a conventional matter. For they reflect the understanding we have of the world. We cannot enlarge that understanding without extending the range of concepts we possess. To take an obvious example, we cannot come to an understanding of Freudian psychology without acquiring rather different concepts from those we already possess. Learn-ing to see human behaviour in Freudian terms involves learn-ing how to employ such concepts as 'repression', 'super-ego', and so on. These concepts are not, of course, unrelated to concepts we already possess, such as 'putting something out of one's mind' or 'conscience'. But they are not reducible to them. And if we accept that a Freudian understanding of human behaviour provides us with "insight" into it, we shall say that it enables us to recognize facts which we would not formerly have been able to accept as such.

It may seem that this argument points to the thesis that *matter-of-fact* claims always *presuppose* the truth of some *grammatical* claim or other. In one obvious sense of "presuppose", however, it would be incorrect to say this. In that sense of "presuppose", one proposition presupposes the truth of the other if, and only if, the truth of the latter is a necessary condition of the truth of the former. But *matter-of-fact* claims cannot be said to "presuppose" the truth of *grammatical* claims in the sense just indicated. For *grammatical* claims provide the context in which *true or false matter-of-fact claims alike* may be made. It is the possibility of a claim's being *either* true or false as a matter of fact which depends on the truth of some grammatical claim or other. For grammatical claims specify the relevant features of a conception of reality whose limits mark the limits of what can intelligibly be claimed.

There are, it may be said, two different kinds of advance in knowledge. One of them, which *consists* in the acquisition of new pieces of information, takes place only *within* an accepted conception of reality. It involves, that is to say, no alteration of the conceptual apparatus in terms of which experience is understood. It would seem reasonable to suppose that advances in knowledge are mostly of this kind. But they are not invariably of this kind. There is another kind which *makes possible* the finding of new information by providing a change in, or extension of, concepts already available. It is, first and foremost, an advance in understanding. But to recognize it as an "advance" is to acknowledge that it makes possible a use of concepts in terms of which new facts could be stated or discovered. Such an advance in understanding involves a change in the accepted conception of reality. For it involves coming to find intelligible what formerly did not make sense to one.

It seems, then, that grammatical claims are presupposed by the possibility of there being knowledge at all. It could not, for instance, be a "fact" whether or not a given sequence of events constituted a "miracle" unless something is *counted* as constituting a "miracle". A man could only claim to know that something was miraculous if he was in a position to exclude as satisfied all reasonable grounds there might be for doubt. An account of what these grounds might be would be a contribution to the grammar of the term "miracle". Many considerations of a grammatical nature must be taken for granted in speaking of "knowledge" in this or any other context. A common language makes it possible for us to take them for granted. For in learning a language we learn when we are, and when we are not, entitled to use a wide range of terms. It is only when we are confronted with new language that the kind of grammatical considerations which commonly remain in the background come to the fore.

If, however, claiming to know something involves claiming that no room for reasonable doubt remains with regard to it, it would seem to follow that only matter-of-fact claims can be *known* to be true. It would follow, that is to say, that grammatical claims could *not* be known to be true. For if it makes no sense to *doubt* whether a given claim is true it equally makes no sense to claim to *know* that it is true.[11] Both doubt and knowledge are out of place with respect to matters of grammar. The question is: Can we still speak of truth and falsity in such matters?

This much may be conceded to the falsifiability requirement, that there could not be a language in which claims could not be made which complied with it. A language *must*, that is to say, embody matter-of-fact claims. It could not otherwise be a statement-making language. Without grammar we should not be able to recognize any matter-of-fact claim as true. Yet it is

[11] This is a point much insisted upon by Wittgenstein in opposition to those philosophers who wished to suggest that we may be more certain in our knowledge of our own sensations than any other matter of fact. Wittgenstein wished to deny that it makes sense for a man to claim to know that he is in pain. See *Philosophical Investigations*, Sect. 246.

because we speak of truth or falsity in relation to matters of fact that we are impelled to do likewise in relation to matters of grammar.

The dilemma posed at the end of the previous section may be met by grasping its first horn. We may, that is to say, deny that it is a condition of rational discussion of the merits of two competing grammatical claims that such claims should be falsifiable in the way required. Reasons can be given for preferring one such claim to another, though they must, in the nature of the case, stop short of being compelling. This is not to say that it is a characteristic of those grammatical claims which reflect a man's understanding of the world that they are endorsed by him only with reservation. For in so far as he can only say to himself "How could it be otherwise?" in a rhetorical way there is no place in such a context for any reservation of a straightforward kind. He may qualify his acceptance only with some vague phrase like "unless I have misunderstood matters". There are indeed matters of grammar concerning which even this qualification seems inappropriate. For example, philosophical accounts of perception have invariably concurred in assuming that experience involves a temporally successive order of perceptions and sensations. This might be called an agreement in grammar. Yet it is not a matter concerning which it is possible to make sense of dissension.

Many questions of grammar are indeed philosophical questions. The question, for example, whether all objects are spatially related to one another is a question about what it makes sense to say. But the question whether it is possible for there to be two objects which are spatially unrelated to one another is one to which many considerations are relevant. Nor is it immediately clear whether or not the supposition that there are two such objects is an intelligible one. For it is not immediately clear what further must be supposed if such a possibility is to be entertained. Whatever position one adopts on such a matter as this, one does not provide for falsification in the way one cannot avoid doing in adopting a position about a matter of fact. But no philosopher has in practice supposed that there is no room for rational discussion of such matters.

Wittgenstein once remarked: "A dog cannot be a hypocrite, but neither can he be sincere." He once asked whether a dog could pretend and followed this question with another: "Is he too honest?" His point in doing so is rhetorical. Were it otherwise, the force of the words "cannot" and "can" would be similar to that of the word "incapable" in the sentence "He was a person incapable of hypocrisy". The "cannot" in "A dog cannot be a hypocrite" is a *grammatical* and not a *matter-of-fact* "cannot". It indicates what it makes sense to say about dogs. But it seems a matter of little interest *that* this is true. What is interesting is *why* it is true. An answer to this question will be a contribution to the philosophy of mind. It may also serve to bring out that the preference which we have for established grammar is by no means unfounded. We may allow this without being committed to deny that this preference is fallible.

VII

RELIGION AND SUPERSTITION

We have seen, in the previous chapter, that some objectivity requirements must be met by any discourse in which claims are made that something is, or is not, the case. This keeps open the possibility of epistemological criticism of an area of discourse on the ground that such requirements are not met in it. We must now ask: How, and on what terms, can such criticism be made?

21. THE SCOPE OF NORMATIVE EPISTEMOLOGY

We have considered *five* of the kinds of account which have been put forward regarding the nature of the apparent intelligibility gap between believer and non-believer. It has been objected to these kinds of account that they cannot be justifiably given *in principle*. For they have either depended on there being quite general standards for deciding what it makes sense to say; or they have depended on there being standards which were, at any rate, quite generally applicable within a given society at a given time. Those forms of S-thesis which involve dismissing religion holus-bolus as superstition have generally relied upon the former kind of consideration. And were these the only forms of S-thesis, such a thesis would not deserve separate consideration. For the S-thesis would stand or, as I believe, fall with the form of U-thesis upon which it relied.

There remains, however, another form of S-thesis which is not open to this kind of objection. It is a thesis about religious claims which, unlike these others, is not objectionable *in principle*. If it is untenable, it is because it cannot be worked out in practice. For it may be possible, by examination of the arguments employed by religious apologists, to *locate* the standards of rationality and intelligibility to which their claims are subject and by which they may in fact be judged. Now if it were possible to establish, with regard to such claims, that they were both irrational and unintelligible when judged by those standards, some basis for an S-thesis would have been established. The adoption of this line of epistemological criticism is quite compatible with the rejection of any *holus-bolus* attempt to employ wholly alien standards in assessing the claims made in a given area of discourse. Indeed, it seems the only line which is left for the normative epistemologist to pursue. It will demand careful study of the way in which arguments are actually advanced and some kind of formal grasp of the concepts involved in them.

This point may be introduced with a simple example. There is a country saying: "We must have March sometime, if not in March." For the man who wishes to pass as weather-wise, it has certain attractions. Given that a period of suitably blustery weather is very likely indeed at some point in the spring or summer months, he is adopting a virtually invulnerable position. For even if he has to wait till June before a characteristically March day comes along, he may still round upon others with his "What did I tell you?" But a price is paid for appearing to be profoundly right when one has run but a negligible risk of being wrong. The price is that of intelligibility. If what is meant were that we always have blustery weather at some time during the spring or summer months, it would command little attention. True, that is what is accepted as confirmation. But it is the introduction of the words "must" and "March" which confer upon the adage its air of profundity. Yet no licence is produced for using the word "must" and the word "March" is in effect freed from the rules which normally govern its use. Such vagueness does not make it easy to distinguish between what one would like to say and what one is entitled to say in such a case. To that extent the adage has the look of a superstition.

This is, however, only a single claim and not a whole area of discourse. It does not presuppose a complex of grammatical claims. It does involve a distinctive claim about the grammar of the word "March", namely, that "March" may occur at other times than March. An area of discourse, on the other hand, involves a complex of grammatical claims which hang together in a certain way. The kind of principle of unity which may be involved in distinguishing one area of discourse[1] from another may perhaps best be brought out by a consideration of examples.

One example, which has already been introduced briefly in Section 3 above, is that of discourse about Fate. It seems to be possible to elaborate something like a Fatology which sets out the terms in which we are supposed to understand events whose outcome lies beyond our control. Such popular adages as "Fortune favours the brave" or "Pride comes before a fall" reflect, it might be said, an awareness of the way in which Fate operates. For it is a characteristic of Fate to intervene in favour of the courageous man and against the arrogant. A man who has had a lucky escape in attempting a difficult climb may be said to be "tempting Providence" if he makes the attempt again. For, it would be said, some presumption is involved in

---

[1] Those familiar with Wittgenstein's later writings may detect a similarity between an "area of discourse" and Wittgenstein's "language-game". My main reason for avoiding the term "game" is that it suggests a conventionalist position. Yet Wittgenstein says, for example, that to accept a proposition as unshakeably certain means "to use it as grammatical rule" (*Remarks on the Foundations of Mathematics*, II 39). Indeed he sometimes speaks as if a grammatical rule was a matter of arbitrary convention in the way in which a rule in a game is. At the end of his lectures on religious belief, he raises the following (grammatical) question: "Are eyebrows going to be talked of, in connection with the Eye of God?" The religious person, he suggests, makes use of a picture, but he does not draw from it all the consequences which the picture may itself point to. He speaks of these consequences as "conventions" which are drawn by religious persons (*Wittgenstein: Lectures and Conversations* (ed. C. Barrett, p. 72). There may therefore be some irony in my adoption of the term "grammar". Yet many of Wittgenstein's examples and other remarks have seemed to me to point firmly away from a conventionalist position. I have continued to use the term since its appropriateness does not depend on whether my use of it accords wholly with that of Wittgenstein.

so doing of a kind which spells ill-fortune to come. And so we might go on.

Now a man who does not believe in Fate, who does not find talk about "tempting Providence" intelligible, may still be able to acquire some grasp of the concepts employed within this area of discourse. He understands well enough what is being claimed if an event is said to be such that no human contrivance could have brought it about. Suppose that it transpires to be a feature of such belief that certain courses of action are thought to guarantee avoidance of misfortune and others to ensure good fortune. Suppose that saying "God-willing" when declaring an intention to do something hazardous is seen as a means of avoiding retribution for being presumptuous. These practices may be seen as means which are directed towards attaining a desired, or avoiding an undesired, end. They may, that is to say, be assessed as causal beliefs.

So regarded, it becomes pertinent to ask whether there is a significant correlation between engaging in such practices or exhibiting the relevant moral qualities and attaining or avoiding certain ends. It becomes pertinent for someone to hold that it made no sense to claim such a spurious causal connection as is here alleged. It may, that is to say, be seen as a set of beliefs which are both irrational and unintelligible judged by the standards which seem to be appropriate, i.e. the standards by which we judge causal claims. Yet it is only as a kind of causal claim that any semblance of intelligibility accrues to the claim that by saying "God-willing" in declaring an intention one does something to enhance the prospect of being successfully able to carry it out. On this account, belief in Fate is a superstition.

In this case, however, we may be mistaken in supposing that the belief and practices involved should be construed in causal terms. For in so far as it is important to express such views in religious terms (e.g. "tempting Providence"), it may be that they should be understood as involving a perversion of Christian belief in Providence. It derives, that is to say, what intelligibility it has from orthodox Christian belief. Yet it does not make sense, in Christian terms, to speak of Providence being "tempted". Nor would it be reasonable for a Christian to expect to be rewarded *in the outcome* of a hazardous enterprise by virtue of the courageous way he embarks upon it. The belief in Fate, at any rate in recent European society, would seem to be a superstition even by religious standards.

Now there are those who will object at this point that belief in Providence is *itself* a form of superstition. I do not wish to rule out the possibility that this may indeed be so. What I am concerned to do here, rather, is to indicate what would *count* as showing this to be the case. I shall try to bring out what it is for a belief to be superstitious with regard to two cases which, unlike that of Fatology, are not of my own contriving.

22. DESCRIPTIVE EPISTEMOLOGY AND SUPERSTITION

I have been arguing against the over-hasty imposition of extraneous norms of intelligibility on religious (or indeed any other) claims. I have, however, argued in favour of the possibility of epistemological criticism of religious claims. But this, I have said, is only possible if some spadework is done to discover the norms to which such claims are actually subject. And this spadework will involve what might be termed "descriptive" epistemology. It makes use of the leverage provided by the concern apologists have to justify their beliefs. For the arguments produced in support of such beliefs will afford some indication of the standards by which they may be judged. And, in so doing, they may betray the superstitious character of the beliefs in question.

It is indeed a characteristic of many contemporary superstitions that they are advocated as legitimate branches of scientific inquiry wrongly outlawed by a biassed scientific establishment. It is in this manner that astrology is defended by one of its prominent British advocates, R. C. Davison.[2] His book is primarily concerned with what is known as "natal astrology", i.e. with "the study of nativities and their relation-

[2] *Astrology*, London (Arco Publications) and New York (Arco Publishing Co.) 1963.

ship to the character and experiences of the individual". The author claims to show how "the astrological principles represented by the planets may effectively be related to the study of human character and behaviour" (p. 14). Such a view would generally be regarded as scientifically unintelligible. Davison himself admits that scientific opinion "inclines to the view that astrology is an outworn superstition of the middle ages" (p. 7). Against this he points out that "many of the so-called experts who have denied the validity of astrology have made no attempt whatever to study the subject". And such an omission, he thinks, "renders them liable to be charged with intellectual dishonesty" (p. 7).

If, however, the terms in which astrological principles are set up are less than satisfactory, there may be some excuse for failure to consider their detailed working. And this, to judge by Davison's attempt to offer a "rational explanation" of the "validity" of astrology, may well be so. For he tries to make use of two kinds of argument, which appear to be in conflict with each other. On the one hand, he appeals to metaphysical argument *against* the senses, claiming that "the sages of earlier times sought to show that the world of phenomena was only a most imperfect and highly misleading manifestation of that which lay beneath" (p. 7f.). On the other hand, he attempts to justify astrology as a science, thus making use of the evidence provided *by* the senses. He claims, for example, that it has been "observed" that

> maximum sun-spot activity takes place . . . when Mars, Jupiter and Saturn are either in a straight line or at right angles to each other, positions recognized in astrology as producing the maximum amount of stress! (p. 10)

Astrology, according to Davison, is the "science of correspondences". It is thus based upon empirical data, since these correspondences are to be established by means of observation. But one seems to be allowed a generous margin of freedom in interpreting what "correspondences" are significant and what not. Davison himself, at any rate, is pretty indulgent on this score. For example he writes as follows:

One of the most striking pieces of evidence in favour of astrology is the fact that those born at the same moment of time and in approximately the same place have a life pattern that is very similar. Not all cases of twin births fulfil these conditions as one twin is often *some minutes older* than the other.... On the day Queen Wilhelmina of the Netherlands married only one other woman in the country was allowed to marry. She was a friend of the Queen, her name too was Wilhelmina and she was *born on the same day* as the queen! (p. 10, my italics.)

The kind of partiality in handling of evidence involved in this passage seems to be an almost blatant violation of the objectivity requirement. For a matter of *minutes* between the birth of twins is sufficient to dismiss the apparently *unfavourable* evidence of different life-histories. Yet, when it comes to finding *favourable* evidence, it is sufficient that two people should be born *on the same day*! Davison seems to adopt a position just like our man who says "We must have March sometime, if not in March", only it seems even more impregnable. But the price, as we have noted, of running no risk of error is that of abandoning the prospect of being right. We are supposed to be impressed by the way in which these "correspondences" hold *as a matter of fact*. It is this which is supposed to cry out for that special kind of explanation natal astrology purports to offer. But unless the evidence is presented impartially, no case will have been made out for supposing that there are correlations which need to be investigated.

However, scepticism about astrology does not rest solely on an inclination to believe that such a case could not be made out. It derives also from regarding it as unintelligible to suppose that the planets could make any difference to human character or human affairs. Davison offers an explanation which is designed to counter the prejudices of those who think astrology is "an outworn superstition of the middle ages". He goes so far as to present it as scientifically valid. It is no impertinence, therefore, to consider his argument as a piece of scientific reasoning. He suggests that the influence of the planets on human behaviour may be accounted for by reference to the effects of radiation on the Earth's atmosphere. This results in cellular changes in the human body. Here he goes on:

Such cellular change must also affect the glands, and the behaviour of these organs is recognized by psychologists as having a bearing on human behaviour. The effect of the Moon on the tides is well known and the combined pull of the luminaries, occurring at the New and Full Moon, is recognized as having the greatest effect upon the oceans of the world. As man's blood closely resembles sea-water in its chemical make-up, it is difficult to resist the conclusion that it too may be subject to the "pull" of the luminaries (p. 11).

This account does indeed confer on astrology a semblance of intelligibility. For the notion of 'pull' is extended to cover 'astrological influence'. But this is a pseudo-explanation. It goes no way towards explaining how the gravitational influence of Mars should affect one person more than another. Nor does it show how the gravitational "pull" of Mars on a man should make him aggressive, or the "pull" of Venus make him amorous. It serves to confirm the suspicion that astrology is a superstition, rather than allay it. For not only is it unreasonable to believe, on the grounds offered by Davison, that there is any correlation between a man's "nativity" and his future life; but his account of this supposed correlation is unintelligible by the standards to which it pretends to be subject. Indeed Davison's account, in using the notion of 'gravitational pull' to confer a pseudo-intelligibility on that of 'astrological influence', exemplifies a further feature of a superstition. For, as he presents it, astrology can only be tempting as a misunderstanding of science just as belief in Fate can only be tempting as a misunderstanding of Providence. Like belief in Fate, it is (as presented by Davison) a parasite on the very orthodoxies from which it is a departure. For in each case it is the orthodox account which confers on the superstition what sense it has.

It needs hardly to be said that my arguments do not show astrology to be a superstition. For it is clear that the terms in which Davison attempts to defend belief in astrological influences cannot have been those in which it has traditionally been presented. It may be thought that no contemporary attempt to make astrology plausible would fare any better than Davison's. But that would be too large a claim to investigate here. It may even be the case that Davison himself has better arguments for his case than he gives. But *if* the piece of "descriptive" epistemology just offered does not distort his arguments *and if* these are the arguments which lead him to believe in astrological influences, the strength of our conclusion may compensate for its lack of breadth. We can say not only that *we* do not find his account unintelligible, but that it *is* unintelligible. And that means Davison cannot make sense of it either.

This is the kind of conclusion which normative epistemologists have sought for religion as a whole. My arguments do not rule out such a conclusion *a priori*. But neither do they allow it to be drawn *a priori*. There are no short-cuts to this kind of conclusion.

23. CHRISTIANITY AND SUPERSTITION

Those who wish to advance an S-thesis with regard to religious claims as a whole are faced with this problem: In relation to what standards of intelligibility can they be represented as such? For it seems that, if one looks at the arguments advanced for religious belief, they seem to depend on considerations which only a believer would be inclined to accept. We are invited, for example, to read and to recognize the authority of that body of writings known as "The Bible". There seems to be a kind of self-sufficiency about the language of religion. Some grasp of its concepts is possible for the unbeliever, but not such as would enable him to recognize the claims of religion as true.

It is possible for the unbeliever to be able to exercise the concepts of religion sufficiently well to make what are, for him, theological *moves*. He may be brought to recognize that, for example, the Black Mass is a practice which can only be understood as a perversion of the Christian sacraments. He may be able to see that such a practice does not make sense except when seen in these terms. For it is the Christian devil, if one may so speak, with whom the pact is made. He may see also that such a pact is a kind of bizarre analogue of communion with God. Such an understanding enables him to see such a practice as superstitious in terms of norms he does not share.

He may think, however, that this conceptual self-sufficiency is itself as damaging to religion as any epistemological criticism of it could hope to be. For what relation can religion have to human life if the language of religion is so isolated from the language in terms of which human experience is otherwise understood? The religious believer seems to be caught between making his religion into an isolated feature of his life and trying to relate it to the language in which his experience is otherwise described. Theologians like Barth are often accused of encouraging such isolationism, albeit unintentionally. But, once it is abandoned, the hazards are considerable.

One contemporary Christian thinker, John Wren-Lewis, has been particularly adventurous in attempting to avoid the dangers involved in treating the language of religion as self-sufficient. Indeed he has, in his lecture entitled "Does science destroy belief?"[3] gone so far in the other direction as to expose himself to the criticism that he presents religious belief as a superstition. It may be instructive to see how he does this. For we shall then have a model of what it would be like for religion as a whole to be a superstition.

Wren-Lewis argues that the Christian view of resurrection, as traditionally presented, must be considered as a "myth". It presents the resurrection of a person as "the survival of some occult part of the personality called the 'soul' in some other world behind the scenes called 'heaven'" (p. 42f.). But quite apart from its unacceptability to modern ways of thinking, such an account is not even true to the early Christian idea. Rather he thinks that

> the general line of the actual findings of modern science make it quite reasonable to take the New Testament idea of *physical* resurrection quite seriously, if we look at them in the *spirit* of modern science (p. 43).

[3] Published in *Faith, Fact and Fantasy*, London (Collins Fontana Books) 1964.

It seems that Wren-Lewis does mean what he says here, that it is findings of modern science which "make it quite reasonable" to accept this idea. It is not, for example, any argument drawn from religion itself. He does not actually put physical resurrection forward as a scientific hypothesis. But it is a conclusion which science points to. Here the phrase "in the *spirit* of modern science" is the operative one. It is a question of interpreting the results of experimental and other scientific inquiry in the right way. The following passage brings out the direction which he considers such an interpretation should take:

> . . . we now have definite evidence from physiology that the body's mechanisms for preserving its vitality and integrity are much stronger than we ordinarily realize, so there is no difficulty in imagining that they may be made to prevent ageing and to resist even major acts of violence (like crucifixion). Moreover if this were to happen, the result would not merely be *everlasting* life: people's whole experience of time would change, since we now know that the sense of time comes from measuring our cyclical processes against the base-line of our general non-reversible growth. There is also some evidence from psychoanalysis that we suffer boredom only because we unconsciously see passing time as bringing us ever closer to death. So everlasting life would be *eternal* life, a life in which time and space would seem like opportunities rather than as overwhelming realities before which people must bow. . . . (p. 43)

Let us take for granted, for the sake of argument, the "evidence" presented from physiology and psychoanalysis. Let us allow too, for the sake of argument, that it could be shown[4] that our concept of temporal direction does presuppose some concept of non-reversible processes. The question is: Have these considerations any tendency to confer scientific plausibility on the suggestion of physical resurrection? Here there is a conspicuous gap in Wren-Lewis' argument. When he says "if this were to happen" it is not clear whether he is saying: (*a*) that ageing processes might be halted *altogether*; or merely (*b*) that death might be postponed for a considerably

---

[4] Wren-Lewis refers in this connection to an article by K. C. Denbigh entitled "Thermodynamics and the subjective sense of time" in the *British Journal for the Philosophy of Science* for November 1953 (vol. iv, no. 15).

longer time than has been realized. The evidence he cites would seem to support the latter thesis (*b*). Yet it is (*a*) which needs to be established for the purposes of the argument. To establish (*a*), Wren-Lewis would need to produce a great deal more argument than he advances here. But if he is content with (*b*), then the consequence is not as he suggests. For his speculation about everlasting life as opposed to eternal life requires our ceasing to be aware of non-reversible processes *at all*.

There is another non-sequitur here. On Wren-Lewis' account, it would seem sufficient to alter "people's whole experience of time" that the human body should not be subject to non-reversible ageing processes. But this would surely not be enough. For as long as there were *any* non-reversible processes, we could still—on the reasoning being accepted—retain our concept of temporal direction.

It might be thought that what Wren-Lewis is trying to do here is to *reconcile* the Christian view of resurrection with scientific developments. But this seems not to be so. He does not, that is to say, give any indication that belief in resurrection might have *other* grounds than the one he provides. On the contrary, he holds that "the idea of resurrection might well be an expression of the ultimate achievements of technology" (p. 43). But not only does Wren-Lewis fail to show it to be reasonable that there might be physical resurrection, he does not even make it intelligible. For, if he must claim that ageing processes may be halted altogether, it sounds as if he is undermining thermodynamics.

Wren-Lewis seems to want, not just a religion which scientists can reasonably be expected to accept, but a *science-based* religion. For example, he invokes Freud in support of his claim that much of traditional religion is an escape from reality. He thinks such sweeping condemnation is all right, since the Old Testament prophets were no less sweeping. But, unlike those prophets, who began by saying "Thus saith the Lord...", Wren-Lewis' position rests on a wholesale acceptance of Freudian views of religion. He dismisses traditional forms of worship as "too loaded with the neurotic associations of the past to be of any use at all" (p. 44). What is "neurotic" about traditional religion, however, is its pre-occupation with a reality *behind* the world of phenomena. True religion, by contrast, must be based upon experience and not avoid its impact (p. 28). What Wren-Lewis claims to offer is "*an experimental counterpart of religious belief*, on the basis of which religion can be fulfilled just as science has been fulfilled" (p. 32).

Wren-Lewis seems in these passages to be trying to make the Christian religion intelligible in wholly secular terms. In doing so he comes at least dangerously close to representing it as a pseudo-scientific superstition. For if the only sense which the idea of physical resurrection could be given were that which he tries to give it, there would be reason to regard it as wholly superstitious. Such a belief would be both irrational and unintelligible by the standards to which, as presented by Wren-Lewis, it pretends to be subject.

Few, however, would be tempted to identify the doctrine which Wren-Lewis seeks to defend with that of the New Testament. Neither would it be generally supposed that such a method of defence provides it with the only kind of basis it could have. On the contrary, the orthodox have always insisted on a resurrection of *the dead*. For them, the *avoidance* of death which is involved in Wren-Lewis' gloss on the notion of 'eternal life' is not part of the Christian hope.

The avoidance of death would indeed be in some respects antagonistic to the traditional view, for reasons given in the following letter from Paul:

So it is with the resurrection of *the dead*. What is sown is perishable, what is raised is imperishable. It is sown in dishonour, it is raised in glory. It is sown in weakness, it is raised in power. *It is sown a physical body, it is raised a spiritual body* (I Cor. 15. v. 42ff., R.S.V., my italics).

This example may serve to illustrate what it would be like for a religion to *become* a superstition. For, like Davison, Wren-Lewis is too ready to accommodate his account to prevailing norms of intelligibility without bringing out how it may be

regarded otherwise than as subject to those norms. He, however, may be credited with attempting to avoid the danger
involved in not relating religious discourse at all to the language
in which men otherwise understand their experience. The
danger is that of isolating the practice of religion from daily
life. But religion is not a set of metaphysical beliefs in some
way connected with a set of liturgical practices. It is a way of
life. It would be quite wrong to recognize this fact by adding a
system of morality which is itself intelligible in secular terms.
For there is no more reason for supposing that religious *behaviour* can be made intelligible in non-religious terms than
that religious *belief* can be. This is obvious enough with praying,
blessing and crossing oneself. An unbeliever could go through
the appropriate motions. He may act the part of a saint in a
play. But he would be in the same difficulty in knowing what
he was doing in going through these motions, if indeed he
could be said to be doing anything more than making certain
movements.

More problematically, however, it seems that the Christian
concepts of, for example, 'love' and 'forgiveness' are neither
identical with nor unrelated to those which are involved in
everyday language (See Section 26 below). If this is so, then it
would seem that we must refer to the language of religion in
order to identify correctly a piece of religious behaviour as
falling under a given description. For if we adopt non-religious
norms for identifying a piece of religious behaviour, we will
have to rely on a U-thesis or a C-thesis to do so. But the
difficulties which beset theses of this kind in relation to the
claims of religion apply equally to them in relation to *descriptions*
offered of religious behaviour. The case for saying that religious
claims are subject to norms implicit in the language of religion
is the same case as that for saying that the norms by which
religious behaviour is correctly to be identified are to be found
in the language of religion.

It follows from this that where an S-thesis *could* be established
with regard to a belief it would have application also to the
practices connected with that belief. If it could, *per improbabile,*

be shown that belief in a God is the product of a hankering after a father-figure, it may then be correct to describe, for example, petitionary prayer as an irrational attempt to get one's desires fulfilled. But the belief in question would have to be shown first to be both irrational and unintelligible. For unless it is irrational it would be inappropriate to account for it in causal terms. And unless it is unintelligible by standards to which it can be shown to be subject, no case can be made for understanding it in another way from the way in which it is understood by those who subscribe to it. I have tried to indicate on what terms such an S-thesis might be advanced. To advance it on the strength of theses about human nature would be to lay oneself open to the objections made earlier in Chapter II.

If we allow, as I should be inclined to do, that there is no means of establishing an S-thesis with regard to, e.g., Christianity taken as a whole, then we will have to allow some independence to the language of religion from the norms of intelligibility to which other claims may be subject. Yet, as is emphasized by allowing distinctive norms for identifying religious behaviour, there must be some relation between the language of religion and the language in which human experience is otherwise understood. A careful course must therefore be steered between *isolating* religious language from and *assimilating* it to the terms in which we ordinarily understand our experience. I shall consider the question as to *what* relation holds between religious and everyday language in Section 31. The question as to what kind of distinctiveness may be claimed for the language of religion will form the topic of the following chapter.

VIII

FAITH AND UNDERSTANDING

THE ARGUMENT of this essay has centred upon the attempt to give an adequate account of the apparent intelligibility gap between the religious believer and the non-believer. On the face of it, the religious believer seems to be committed to claims which he (presumably) finds intelligible. Yet these claims are not found intelligible by the non-believer. Some of the accounts we have considered have cited the reason why religious claims do not make sense to the non-believer as, quite simply, that they do not make sense. If an adequate foundation could be laid for any such account—i.e. for a U-thesis or a C-thesis—the intelligibility gap could be dismissed as *merely* apparent. But such a foundation cannot be provided. This of itself would equally deprive R-theses or D-theses of any basis. They represent the gap as more than merely apparent, in so far as their programmes are designed to close it. But such programmes are open to the objection that they cannot preserve identity of belief. Nor can an adequate basis be found for a P-thesis on the side of epistemology, if religious claims which are not falsifiable may be construed as "grammatical" in character.

The only way, then, in which we could avoid having to accept this intelligibility gap as a *necessary* feature of the relation between believer and non-believer would be to develop the form of S-thesis against the religion in question which has been considered in the previous chapter. If we cannot do this, we shall be forced to accept that some B-thesis is correct with regard to that religion. We shall, in other words, have to accept both the genuine character of the gap and the distinctive character of that religion's language. The question remains, *what form* of B-thesis could be maintained. I shall consider this question in the context of the Christian religion. In the language of that religion, it may be presented as a problem about faith and understanding. But though this problem has a theological dimension, it is with its epistemological aspect that I shall here be concerned.

24. SOME EPISTEMOLOGICAL ACCOUNTS OF FAITH

Faith has commonly been understood as assent to something there is no reason for believing. Matters of faith have been contrasted with matters of fact in such a way as to suggest that faith is in some way irrational and blind. This has given rise to the view that one man's opinion on such matters as religion is as good as the next's. If both are equally defensible, it is because both are equally indefensible. On such matters reason is assumed to have been left behind.

Religious apologists, not surprisingly, have often been anxious to correct such an assumption. Alan Richardson, for example, has tried to do so by developing Augustine's view that faith is itself what makes understanding possible. He opposes the view of faith as a doubtful end-product of reasoning which is at best tendentious. Rather, he writes;[1]

> Faith for St Augustine is not intellectual assent to certain scriptural propositions; it is the awakening of the mind to truth, a new way of seeing things, a means of understanding what before did not make sense, the acquiring of categories of interpretation by means of which our whole experience and thought become rational and coherent.

Richardson's suggestion that faith is "not a substitute for understanding but a condition of it" (p. 235) makes his version of B-thesis not unlike that offered by Zuurdeeg. While Richardson speaks of "faith-principles" as necessarily being involved in any attempt at understanding the universe, Zuurdeeg says that "convictional elements" (APR 47ff.)

[1] *Christian Apologetics*, London (SCM Press) and New York (Harper & Row) 1947, p. 238.

are an inevitable feature of any inquiry. Richardson says that "we must be on our guard against the intellectualist fallacy of supposing that a faith or a key-idea can be selected as a result of a purely rational and 'objective' examination of 'facts' " (p. 37). But this of itself does not commit him to a relativist position. His handling, however, of the question about truth in relation to his thesis is somewhat bland:

> Man comes to the knowledge of the truth, not by the untrammelled exercise of his reasoning powers, but by accepting or being given the faith which enables him to use his reason aright; reason cannot work until it first makes an act of faith, and it does not work correctly—that is, rationally—unless it makes the *right* act of faith, unless it has faith in the Truth itself. Reason does not precede faith, as rationalism supposes, but faith precedes reason (p. 77).

If, however, Richardson avoids Zuurdeeg's difficulties, his account has problems of its own. In particular his account of belief as a *condition* of understanding (*credo ut intelligam*) is presented in such a way that it looks as if the "leap" of faith has to be made at a time when the believer does not yet understand. But if that is so, how does he know in what direction he is leaping? To put the point without the metaphor: How can one call something a *belief* if the person to whom it is ascribed does not *understand* what it is he is believing? It is one thing to say that a Christian's understanding of his faith can only be deepened and enlarged by persevering in it. It is quite another thing to say to the unbeliever: "Unless ye believe, ye shall not understand." For the unbeliever's problem is that he does not know where to start. He does not know, that is, what it is he is being asked to believe. Some understanding must therefore be involved in faith itself. A viable form of B-thesis must provide for this feature.

Another form of B-thesis is presented, albeit schematically, by R. M. Hare. He suggests that "*even* our belief in so-called hard facts rests in the end on a faith, a commitment, which is not in or to facts, but in that without which there would not be any facts".[2] It may be that it is in these terms that Hare

[2] *Faith and Logic* (ed. B. Mitchell) London (Allen & Unwin) and Boston (Beacon Press) 1957, p. 192.

intends his talk of "bliks" to be understood. For he says else-where[3] that "our whole commerce with the world depends upon our *blik* about the world". It is by means of such "bliks", he suggests, that we understand our experience. They provide the terms in which our explanations are to be given, for it is by reference to them "that we decide what is and what is not an explanation". This suggests a form of B-thesis which also involves a P-thesis, since Hare denies that articulations of "bliks" are genuine assertions. The difficulty with such a view has already been discussed in another context (See Section 20 above). It is this: How can a matter-of-fact claim be regarded as true if the "blik" by virtue of which it is counted as a matter-of-fact claim is not so regarded?

A rather different form of B-thesis has been more closely developed by Hick. His starting-point is a neo-Kantian thesis that "the perceiving mind is . . . always in some degree a selecting, relating and synthesizing agent" (FK 108). For, he thinks, some element of interpretation must always be present if we are able to make intelligible to ourselves the material provided by our sensory organs. The amount of freedom of interpretation varies. With sense-perception we are particularly restricted, though Hick suggests (contentiously) that we are free to interpret our experience *either* as of "an objective world of enduring, causally interacting objects, which we share with other people" (FK 109), *or else* as of only our immediate sense-impressions in a solipsistic manner. In matters of religion, however, there is considerable freedom of interpretation. Faith, he suggests, is a special case of a "primary and unevidenceable act of interpretation" such as is required if we are to make sense of our experience. It differs from its non-religious ana-logues in being an interpretation of human experience *as a whole*. An act of faith "is not to be described as either a reasoned conclusion or an unreasoned hunch that there is a God. It is, putatively, an apprehension of the divine presence within the believer's human experience" (FK 115).

In speaking of faith as a "primary and unevidenceable act

[3] *New Essays in Philosophical Theology*, p. 101.

of interpretation", Hick seems to suggest that some interpreting process, albeit unconscious and gradual, *had* to precede any experience of the world. On such an account, it must seem very remarkable that members of a given society do very substantially agree in the descriptions which they offer of their experience. Hick cannot adequately explain why this should be so or why being brought up in a different society should make any difference to one's categories of interpretation. Yet it is in no way remarkable that members of one society should agree, and different societies diverge, in the modes of description available to them. For, in acquiring one's mother language one is at the same time acquiring the conception of reality implicit in it. It is a conception of reality which, in the main, is shared by other members of our society. We may come to acquire somewhat different categories of interpretation, as may be provided by religion or political ideology. But this is characteristically part and parcel with joining a sub-group of society which has, to some extent, a language of its own.

Hick's position seems to be wrong in suggesting that something analogous to faith is required in order to have a means of describing one's experience. To insist on such *"acts* of interpretation" on such an *a priori* basis is to engage in what is called "transcendental psychology". But an adequate account of how we come to have the conception of reality we do have may be given without insisting on there being such "acts" whether or not empirical psychology can confirm them. It may be, however, that something like faith is required to *sustain* a conception of reality, as I have suggested might be the case with a man's belief that every event has a natural cause (See Section 19 above). Faith may, therefore, be connected with one's categories of interpretation, as Hick suggests. Indeed it seems as if a B-thesis must hold it to be thus connected in some way.

Hick's emphasis on *"acts* of interpretation" seems to derive from two sources. One is the concern to give an account of 'faith' which will not be irredeemably obscure to the unbeliever. As such, it does succeed in no small way. For the outsider finds the language of religion very much a *construction put upon* experience. For him, it may be that an *act* of interpretation is needed if he is to be able to put the same construction upon his experience. But that is because he has already learnt to speak of his experience in another way.

The other source of Hick's emphasis on *acts* of interpretation seems to be the influence of a particular Christian tradition. It is that which lays great stress on the need for every man to be "born again", to undergo a conversion and take a definite *step* of faith. Hick's account of faith fits well enough into that tradition. But there is a tradition in which "faith" is still spoken of, yet in which no such emphasis is laid on *steps* of faith. Those who adhere to this tradition will say that there is no basis for claiming that those who have been baptized and brought up "in the faith" should subsequently need to be converted to it. It is, of course, a theological matter which side of the "once-born" controversy is right. An epistemological account of 'faith' should leave the controversy where it is. Hick's account, even if not intentionally, makes it very difficult for one side of the controversy to *state* its position. For it obliges them to do so in the language of "transcendental psychology".

The difficulties encountered by these four forms of B-thesis indicate the limits within which one may hope to find epistemological space for this kind of thesis. Against Hare I have insisted that affirmations of faith must be true or false. Against Zuurdeeg I have maintained that one must recognize the pretension to objectivity involved in the claim that something is "true" or "false". Against Hick I have argued that faith cannot be satisfactorily construed as an act. And against Richardson I have claimed that one cannot say that belief *precedes* understanding. But, since it would be contrary to a B-thesis to allow that understanding precedes belief, an account is needed of coming to religious belief in which understanding and belief come together. Only one concept could express coming to a belief in these terms. It is that of 'insight'. In trying to sharpen this concept I have somewhat narrowed its range of application (See Section 12 above). But it is in terms of such a concept, I shall suggest, that one can make epistemological sense of a B-thesis about the nature of the intelligibility gap between believer and unbeliever.

25. BELIEF AND UNDERSTANDING

Such a B-thesis has not, however, been thought free from difficulty. Indeed there seems to be a serious drawback in making belief and understanding go together. For how can one provide in such terms for the possibility of religious belief being rejected? In particular, how is it possible for what is called "loss of faith" to occur? It may look as if the advocates of a B-thesis must deny that anyone ever really rejects *Christianity*. For anyone who *thinks* he has rejected it must, as MacIntyre puts it, "have lacked saving grace and so did not understand Christianity and so in fact rejected something else" (FP 116). Similarly, it seems that a man who has "lost his faith" cannot ever really have had it and must therefore be said to have lost, not his faith, but something else.

However, the possibility of a man's rejecting Christian belief as *false* can be provided for by a B-thesis. Even though he may not know what it is for such beliefs to be true, this does not preclude him from finding them sufficiently intelligible to know what it would be for them to be false. It is, as we saw in connection with belief in Fate (Section 3 above), compatible with finding a belief unintelligible that one should reject it as false. Someone for whom it was, as it were, an article of faith that every event has a natural cause might reject Christianity on the grounds that, as traditionally presented, it has insisted on miracles. It may be true that *he* is not in a position to say whether or not his belief is incompatible with belief in the Immaculate Conception. For it is a *theological* matter what one would be committed to believe in accepting this doctrine. But it may very well turn out to involve a repudiation of the belief that every event had a natural cause. Someone who held this latter belief would then be committed to regarding the doctrine as *both* unintelligible *and* false: *unintelligible*, because he does not know what it would be for it to be true: and *false*, because it is incompatible with what he holds to be true.

The question of "loss of faith" presents greater complications than does that of simple rejection of religious belief. One reason for this is that the concept 'loss of faith' belongs to the language of religion. It is not altogether appropriate, except perhaps in a few cases, for a man whose former co-religionists describe as having "lost his faith" to say this of himself. For the rejection of religion, like its acceptance, has retrospective implications. Just as the convert may retrospectively speak of his former "blindness to the truth", the man who gives up religious belief may describe himself as "having come to see" that his former views were untrue. If a man said he no longer shared Christian insights, we could only make sense of his remark by surrounding the word "insights" with inverted commas. Thus the question whether or not "loss of faith" is possible is ambiguous. It may be raised *independently* of the language of religion. Here it is a question about what is involved in giving epistemological approval to a B-thesis. Alternatively, it may be raised *within* the language of religion.

Firstly, is one committed to denying the possibility of "loss of faith" by allowing that belief and understanding may go together? It is true that one would be providing for such a denial being *itself* possible, as I shall shortly bring out. But it is not true that such an account precludes what, *outside* the language of religion, would be referred to as "loss of faith". On the contrary, in providing epistemological space for a B-thesis with regard to religious claims, we are thereby making the very same provision for anti-religious claims. It is of epistemological interest how insights are to be characterized, i.e. to give an account of the concept 'insight'. The task of commending or criticizing insights is not in general a distinctively philosophical one. Superstitions may involve pseudo-insights, however, and it may be possible for a descriptive epistemologist to expose these for what they are. But the considerations which may be relevant to accepting or rejecting an alleged insight are as varied as the subject-matters in which conceptual change may take place.

Now it is true that the rejection of an insight as such is not, on the view being put forward, compatible with having grasped just what is being suggested. This is true, at any rate, except for those cases where an alleged insight is held to be a pseudo-insight (as with superstitions) where a greater grasp is claimed than that allowed to the person claiming the insight. It is possible to reject a claimed insight without understanding it because it may be possible to recognize its incompatibility with what one is already prepared to accept. One does not need to be able to make sense of the claim that the thoughts of someone in Australia can instantaneously affect those of someone in France without there being any recognized channel of communication between them. One can still reject it as untrue.

A man may come to abandon religion by coming to accept certain anti-religious insights just as he may accept it through endorsing certain religious insights. Some people have, for example, regarded the view that there is "quite pointless evil" in the world as an anti-Christian "insight". Orthodox Christendom has accepted that there *is* evil in the world, but it has commonly[4] been insisted that such evil has to be viewed within the context of God's purpose for the Creation as a whole. We cannot, of course, know this purpose in detail. But it is nevertheless a matter of faith that God would not allow quite pointless suffering to be inflicted on men. The anti-Christian insight would be expressed by the simple allegation that he does allow pointless suffering or that there is such pointless suffering.

Now, in so far as it is a matter of faith, it would seem to make no sense (in the language of the Christian religion) to deny that God would not permit quite pointless suffering. It is this context in relation to which the claim that there *is* such

---

[4] It has been suggested to me that this is a heretical view. If that is so, it would *not* be an anti-Christian "insight" that there is "quite pointless evil" in the world. But the view—heresy or no—is sufficiently widespread to serve an illustrative purpose.

pointless suffering is unintelligible. Someone who makes such a claim is *using* the language of religion in order to say what, *within* the language of religion, cannot intelligibly be said. In doing so he may perhaps be commending a different understanding of evil. For instance, he may be suggesting that it is a *contingent* matter and not a matter of grammar that an evil has any point. But then the "point" which he thinks evil may have will be rather different. He may, for example, consider that there is a point to the suffering brought about by war if lasting peace results from it. If so he must have a different concept of the point which an evil may have from the religious man.

We have considered the question whether "loss of faith" is possible in terms which do not belong to the language of religion itself. In so doing we have spoken of how a man may cease to accept religious beliefs. But the expression "loss of faith" is itself a religious one. The question may therefore be raised, from within the language of religion, whether or not "loss of faith" is possible. It may be profitable to consider this question briefly in order to contrast the external and the internal question. Some theologians have attempted to rule out the possibility of "loss of faith", among them Barth:[5]

> . . . faith is concerned with a decision *once for all*. Faith is not an opinion replaceable by another opinion. A temporary believer does not know what faith is. . . . A man who believes once believes once for all. . . . One may, of course, be confused and one may doubt; but whoever once believes has something like a *character indelibilis.*

Barth's position, as stated, is consistent with two theses. Either (*a*) he is saying that *as a matter of fact* no Christian does ever lose his faith entirely; or else (*b*) he is saying that nothing would *count* as a *believer* losing his faith entirely. Were he endorsing (*a*), one would expect to find at least some factual support for what would then appear a sweeping generalization. Moreover one would expect some hint of what, for Barth, *would* count as a believer's losing his faith. Yet neither of these expectations is

[5] *Dogmatics in Outline* (tr. G. T. Thomson), London (SCM Press) 1949, p. 20 and New York (Harper & Row Torchbooks) 1959.

fulfilled. Barth simply does not contemplate the possibility of a believer's losing his faith. This suggests that (*b*) more accurately represents his position. If this is so, then we may say that it is for Barth *a matter of faith* that the believer cannot lose his faith. This is not, of course, to say that no reason can be given why it does not make sense to say that the believer can lose his faith. It is the object of theology to provide such reasons. But the reasons given will *themselves* depend for their acceptability as good reasons on further statements of faith.

The claim that faith may be tested but cannot be lost seems therefore to be "grammatical" in character. If this is so, then it is possible for the believer to answer the question: "What would have to occur or to have occurred to constitute for you a disproof of the love of, or the existence of, God?"[6] The reply of the orthodox has been: "Nothing can separate us from the love of God." To the philosopher, such an answer may appear at first sight to be wholly inappropriate. But if my arguments have been correct it may be as good an answer as any. For the question is itself the wrong kind of question to ask of matters of faith. It makes indeed precisely the same error as Dr Johnson's celebrated attempt to refute Berkeley by kicking a stone.[7]

26. THEOLOGY AS "GRAMMAR"

Any religion, in so far as it purports to embody a distinctive conception of reality, must embody what I have called "grammatical claims" or what would, in Christian terminology, be called "articles of faith". One purpose of theology is to present

[6] This is the actual wording of the question as put by Flew, *New Essays in Philosophical Theology*, p. 99.

[7] Non-philosophers may not quickly see the force of this point. It might be said that Dr Johnson took the concept 'material substance' to be a straightforward empirical one, hence took Berkeley to be committed to denying, as a matter of fact, that there were, for example, any stones. (See Section 1 above). Philosophers have found more sophisticated reasons for supposing that Dr Johnson did, without realizing it, refute Berkeley's position. For Berkeley's account of causation is in considerable difficulty in accommodating cases where an agent brings about a given result by *doing* something. Dr Johnson's swinging his leg towards the stone might be considered as just such a case.

and interpret those "articles of faith" in a systematic and coherent way. A genuine religion, i.e. one against which an S-thesis cannot successfully be brought, will embody not only grammatical but also matter-of-fact claims. And *these* claims must meet the objectivity requirement. Religion is thus by no means *identical* with theology even where, as in Christianity, its practices are much influenced by it. Whether or not a man is a "saint", whether or not a given course of action is "God's will" for a given man, these are, within the language of the Christian religion, *questions of fact*. Theology may discuss the apparatus in terms of which they can be raised. But it is not a *theological* matter how they should be answered in a given case. Not all religious beliefs could be articles of faith.

I have already tried to indicate how Wittgenstein's suggestion that theology is a kind of *grammar* might be developed (see Section 9 above). This may at first sight seem to be far removed from any traditional understanding of theology. But it is no novelty to point out some marked differences between theological claims and what are more easily recognized as factual claims. As we saw in the previous section, theologians seem more concerned with what *must* be the case than what is— *as a matter of fact*—the case. On Barth's account it is *impossible* for the believer to lose his faith. The question of the epistemological standing of theological claims is closely connected to the question as to what is meant by the word "impossible" in this context. To speak of theology as concerned to articulate the grammar of a religion is to offer one answer to both these questions.

Theologians have concerned themselves with such matters only indirectly. But they have not neglected them. Christian theologians have, for example, agreed that it is in some sense "impossible" for the evil man to escape divine punishment. But a great deal of difference is made by understanding this impossibility in one way rather than another. This may be seen by considering some remarks made by C. H. Dodd and Kierkegaard which are directed against what they view as a *mis*understanding of divine judgment.

The view Dodd and Kierkegaard wish to correct represents the operation of divine justice as involving a kind of cosmic legal system. Within this sytem we are promised retribution for evil done in this life and reward for good done. We may get away with evil-doing in this life, but sooner or later we shall be required to pay the penalty. The good man may suffer ill in this life, but he will be more than compensated in the next. This view is popularly elaborated by the introduction of such officers of the divine court as the "recording Angel".

This monarchical conception of the deity has seemed to be supported by certain of the Biblical writers. The language used by Paul, for example, sometimes suggests that his God is one given to revenge. And this suggests that he is in some way arbitrary in his dealings with men. This understanding of the deity is often defended by insisting that God's wrath is wreaked upon the evil-doer in the name of justice and not revenge. But the impious have sensed that this distinction is not as clear-cut as might at first appear. For, as they have pointed out, God is not thought of as a mere *executive* of divine justice. It is *his* justice—or, as the impious might peevishly put it, *his sense* of justice—which is being appeased by such an administration of reward and punishment. The overtones of arbitrariness attaching to such talk of the justice of God seem difficult to explain away.

Dodd attempts to give an account of Paul's view[8] which will show that it is a "mere caricature" to construe it as representing God as "a vengeful despot". When Paul speaks of "The Wrath" he is, Dodd claims, speaking about the consequences which follow wrong-doing within the "moral order". It is not that God imposes punishment on the wicked from the outside. Rather the "moral order" is such that sin has inevitable consequences. " 'The Wrath of God' . . . , as seen in actual operation, consists in leaving sinful human nature to 'stew in its own juice'."[9] It is true that Paul uses expressions (e.g. "God gave

[8] *The Meaning of Paul for Today*, London 1920, Collins Fontana Books 1958, p. 66ff.
[9] op. cit., p. 67. Dodd cites Romans I vv. 18–32 in support of this claim.

them up . . .'') which suggest special supernatural intervention. But these should, if Dodd is correct, be understood as a manner of speaking. " 'The Wrath' . . . is revealed before our eyes as the increasing horror of sin working out its hideous law of cause and effect" (p. 68).

By speaking of a "moral order" within which certain consequences are inevitable, Dodd is trying to capture the sense of "necessary" in which it is necessary that a man should "pay the price" for his evil-doing. It is clear, however, that he is not claiming any straightforward causal connection. He is not claiming that there is a specific ill which results from specific vices as, for instance, venereal disease results from fornication. The "moral order" seems, that is to say, to be contrasted with the natural order and yet to be in some way analogous to it.

It is not clear, however, that an analogue with *causal* necessity reflects what Dodd himself wishes to say about divine judgment. For there are points at which he wishes to speak of corruption not so much as a *consequence* of sin but as what *constitutes* sin.[10] When someone says to a person who has taken to bouts of heavy drinking, "If you carry on like that you will become a drunkard", he is not speaking of the *effect* of his carrying on with his bouts of drinking but what his so carrying on would *amount* to. This example may in some respects misrepresent the relation between doing sinful acts and falling into sin. But it may serve to indicate that not all talk about the "results" of human behaviour is causal in character. There seems to be a connection which is stronger than causal between sin and the consequences which overtake the sinner. For it could not be a matter of surprise that actions counted as "sinful" had a tendency to produce what is regarded as a "perversion" or "corruption" of human nature. That is, it might be said, precisely what is or should be *meant* by calling those actions "sinful". It is not, in this case, that sin invariably has results

[10] For example, when he says: " 'The judgment' which overtakes sin is the growing perversion of the moral atmosphere of human society, which cannot but affect to a greater or less degree every individual born into it" (p. 68). The force of the "cannot but" here seems to be grammatical rather than causal.

of a particular kind though it might not have. It would, on the contrary, make no sense to speak of "sin" as though the "punishment" for it was something additional which might or might not befall the sinner.

Kierkegaard is at this point clearer. He addresses himself more to the "reward" side of what Dodd terms "the moral order". When the lover saves another human being from death, he writes, there is a sense in which he also saves himself from death. "This he does at the same time; it is one and the same; he does not save the other at one moment and at another save himself, but in the moment he saves the other he saves himself from death."[11] It is in this light that the following passage should be understood:

> The self-lover is busy; he shouts and complains in order to make sure he is not forgotten—and yet he is forgotten. But the lover, who forgets himself, is remembered by love. There is one who thinks of him, and in this way it comes about that the lover gets what he gives.

It is evident that Kierkegaard is not saying that, as a *matter of fact*, the self-lover is forgotten. Had this been his suggestion, it would seem to be a generalization which is at best sweeping and at worst palpably false. It seems equally clear that Kierkegaard is not claiming that, as a *matter of fact*, the lover is remembered by love. For he is expressly ruling out the idea of any *quid pro quo*. His claim that it is in the act of self-forgetfulness that the lover is remembered is a theological claim. To understand it is to understand something of the grammar of the Christian religion. It says something about the Christian concept of love. If one does not share this concept of love one can only find such claims unintelligible. In what some would call "worldly" terms they are indeed unintelligible. If they are true it requires some insight for us to recognize that they are so.

[11] *Works of Love* (tr. H. and E. Hong) London (Collins) and New York (Harper & Row) 1962, p. 262. My attention was drawn to this example by the mention made of it by D. Z. Phillips in his article entitled "Faith, scepticism and religious understanding", RU 75f. Phillips also refers to another example from Kierkegaard which is comparable. (See *Works of Love*, p. 351f.) It concerns what Phillips speaks of as "an internal relation" between forgiving another and being forgiven oneself.

Kierkegaard's thought may without partiality be described as "profound".

It may be objected to the examples given here to bring out the grammatical character of theological claims that they suggest a somewhat non-theistic account of religion. For if the system of rewards and punishments is not to be thought of as imposed externally by a higher being but as in some way internal to the "moral order", then God becomes a subsidiary if not indeed redundant feature of religion. But, it may be thought, there must be something far wrong with the thesis that *all* theological claims are grammatical if it has this consequence. Moreover, there must be at least one claim presupposed by theology which can only be of a matter-of-fact character. That is the claim that God exists. A satisfactory account of the epistemological status of religious affirmations must prove adequate as an account of what is meant by speaking of the "existence" of God. In considering this problem we may hope for further clarification of what case there is for speaking of theology as "grammar".

IX

THE "EXISTENCE" OF GOD

PHILOSOPHERS OF religion have traditionally been concerned
with the merits and demerits of attempts to prove that there
exists a Being a greater than which cannot be thought. They
have, indeed, been concerned to establish or refute the thesis
that such a Being *must* exist. Their arguments have been very
varied and have often been subtle. I shall only discuss two such
arguments. But, though I think they do not succeed, I wish to
criticize what they were seeking to establish rather than their
method of arriving at it. For they seek to establish, as do all
the theistic proofs, a kind of highest common factor of the so-
called "monotheistic" religions, leaving it to the Christian,
Jew or Muslim to argue for his way of filling in the further
details concerning the nature of the deity. I wish to question
the assumptions which underlie belief or disbelief with regard
to the existence of such a deity.

27. DIFFICULTIES IN THEISM

A recent version of the Ontological Argument has been presented by Norman Malcolm[1] and summarized by him in the
following terms:

> If God, a being a greater than which cannot be conceived, does
> not exist then He cannot *come* into existence. For if He did He
> would either have been *caused* to come into existence or have
> *happened* to come into existence, and in either case He would be a

[1] "Anselm's Ontological Arguments", *The Philosophical Review*, January
1960, reprinted in *The Existence of God* (ed. J. Hick) New York (Macmillan)
1964. See p. 56.

limited being, which by our conception of Him He is not. Since He cannot come into existence, if He does not exist His existence is impossible. If He does exist He cannot have come into existence (for the reasons given), nor can He cease to exist, for nothing could cause Him to cease to exist nor could it just happen that He ceased to exist. So if God exists His existence is necessary. Thus God's existence is either impossible or necessary. It can be the former only if the concept of such a being is self-contradictory or in some way logically absurd. Assuming that this is not so, it follows that He necessarily exists.

The conclusion of this argument is that the *proposition* 'God exists' is necessarily true. It is not, that is to say, merely contingently true. But this conclusion is supposed to follow from God's being a wholly non-contingent *being*. These two occurrences of the words "necessary" and "contingent" are, however, quite different. A necessary *being* is one which does not depend on any other being for its existence and does not exist fortuitously. A necessary *proposition*, however, is one which it would be self-contradictory or in some way logically absurd to deny. A transition has been made from *de re* to *de dicto* necessity. Can the transition be made? I think not. For it is compatible with God's being a wholly non-contingent being that he should *cause himself* to go out of existence. Indeed if he were a being greater than which cannot be conceived it would then seem to be necessary that he should *be able* to cause himself to go out of existence. But then it would seem to be a contingent matter that he chooses *not* to do this, and thus a contingent matter that he does actually exist. If this is so, then not only is God's being a necessary being *compatible* with its being a contingent matter whether or not he actually exists, but it *requires* it to be a contingent matter. It would, in other words, be self-contradictory to affirm that it is a necessary truth that a being capable of causing itself to go out of existence exists.

The notion of a 'necessarily existent being' seems to be an absurd one. For either a being has the power to put itself out of existence or it has not. If it has, then it must be a contingent matter that it does not. If it has not, then it is a limited being. But then it is a contingent matter that it is so limited.

Yet the temptation to speak of God as a "necessarily existent

being" is a perennial one. Malcolm is concerned indeed to
capture and express an idea he believes to be "essential to the
Jewish and Christian religions". For him the occurrence of such
an idea in those religions constitutes "a disproof of the dogma,
affirmed by Hume and others, that no existential proposition
can be necessary".

Two questions arise here. Firstly, is it possible for such an
eccentric use of the verb "to exist" to serve as the solitary
counter-example which suffices to refute the Humean "dogma"?
Secondly, is this idea of a 'necessarily existent being' essential,
as Malcolm maintains, to the Jewish and Christian religions?

Malcolm does not think a proof of a necessary existence is
altogether without precedent. He cites the case of Euclid's
demonstration of the existence of an infinity of prime numbers.
There are, he suggests, "as many kinds of existential propositions as there are kinds of subjects of discourse". In a sense this
is true. But the Humean "dogmatist" may point out that these
other uses of the verb "to exist" are not essential. When we say,
for example, that a distinction exists between X and Y, we may
re-express this by saying that it is possible to draw a distinction
between X and Y. When we say, to take one of Malcolm's
examples, "The pain continues to exist in his abdomen", we
could equally well say "He still has a pain in his abdomen".
But when we try to re-phrase such claims as "Unicorns do not
exist" we cannot avoid using existential language. We can say
"There are no unicorns". But if we said "No unicorn has ever
been found" our claim is weakened.

There is, in a sense, no harm in saying that Euclid's proof
establishes the *necessary existence* of an infinity of prime numbers.
We might, by the same licence, say it established the *necessary
non-existence* of a limit to the series of prime numbers. But there
is no harm in such locutions precisely because we have to hand
a range of alternative ways of speaking by means of which the
same point can be made. If someone did not understand what
we meant we could fall back on something like: "No limit can
be drawn to the series of prime numbers". But if there is
an alternative way of speaking about God as other than a

"necessarily existent being", it is not contemplated by Malcolm. It is just this non-availability of an alternative way of speaking which makes talk about a *necessary existence* seem unintelligible *in this case.*

A more hopeful line of argument is that developed by Berkeley. We have briefly alluded to this argument of his already (see Section 1). But it is worth noting the way in which he himself actually presents it:[2]

> ... sensible things cannot exist otherwise than in a mind or spirit. Whence I conclude, not that they have no real existence, but that, seeing they depend not on my thought, and have an existence distinct from being perceived by me, *there must be some other Mind wherein they exist.* As sure, therefore, as the sensible world really exists, so sure is there an infinite omnipresent Spirit who contains and supports it.

Berkeley is here concerned with what must be *presupposed* in claiming *both* that it is "inconceivable" that there should be an idea or sensation not produced in, or by, a mind *and* that sensible things have a real existence independent of *my* thought (or that of other human beings). These are indeed grammatical claims, claims which it would make no sense to deny, on Berkeley's view. His *meta*-grammatical claim that God exists does seem to be presupposed by these claims. If, that is to say, we accept them, we are committed to believing in the existence of an infinite Spirit. It is, it seems, against the premisses of Berkeley's proof of the existence of God that we should direct our criticism if we are unwilling to accept his conclusion. We must dispute his grammatical claims—in particular, his *esse est percipi* principle.

Berkeley's argument is, in effect, designed to show that it is the existence of God (and not, *pace* Locke, that of material substances) which is required by the language of perception. This suggests that it might at least be possible to show that the existence of God was necessary[3] to the language and practice

---

[2] This passage is taken from near the beginning of the Second of his *Three Dialogues between Hylas and Philonous.* See *Berkeley's Philosophical Writings* (ed. D. M. Armstrong), New York (Collier Books) 1965, p. 175.

[3] This line of thought was suggested to me by some remarks D. W. Hamlyn made in an informal paper at Birkbeck College.

of religion. No apologetic purpose would be served by such an argument. But if the claim that God necessarily exists is understood as *meta*-grammatical in character, some light may be thrown on the nature of the *problem* about the "existence" of God. If it is said that it is in some sense a necessary truth (necessary to the language of religion) that God exists, a position is adopted which is analogous to that of Locke. For Locke's account of material substances suggests that, for him, their existence is necessary to the language of perception. It might, therefore, be not unreasonable to expect someone to play the Berkeley to our Locke if we said that God's existence is in this way necessary to the language of the Christian (or other) religion. It is in relation to this expectation that considerable philosophical interest attaches to the way in which John A. T. Robinson construes the well-known anti-theistic views he put forward in his *Honest to God*. He writes[4] of having come, without realizing it,

> to the same sort of point which Bishop Berkeley reached in his questioning of Locke's philosophy of substance. Was it really essential, in order to assert the fact of being held in this inescapable personal relationship as the final interpretative reality of life, to posit this concept of a divine Person behind the scenes?

What Robinson tries to do, albeit sketchily, is to bring out something of what a non-theistic language of religion might be like. And this involves him in re-interpreting what it is theology is about. For, in *some* sense, an atheistic theology is obviously a contradiction in terms. But not in *any* sense. For the adequacy of the accepted concept of 'theos' may itself be questioned. The contradiction may thus be retained, but placed elsewhere. This is just what Robinson does. On his account, an "atheist" (in that sense in which an "atheistic" theology *would* be a contradiction in terms) would be a person who denies that there is any "ultimate reality". He writes:[5]

---

[4] In a sequel, *Exploration into God*, London (SCM Press) and Stanford (Stanford University Press) 1967, p. 22.

[5] *Honest to God*, London (SCM Press) and Philadelphia (Westminster Press) 1963, p. 49f.

A statement is "theological" not because it relates to a particular being called "God", but because it asks *ultimate* questions about the meaning of existence: it asks what, at the level of *theos*, at the level of its deepest mystery, is the reality and significance of our life. A view of the world which affirms this reality and significance in personal categories is *ipso facto* making an affirmation about the *ultimacy* of personal relationships: it is saying that *God*, the final truth and reality "deep down things", *is* love. And the specifically Christian view of the world is asserting that the final definition of this reality, from which "nothing can separate us", since it is the very ground of our being, is "the love of God in Christ Jesus our Lord".

Robinson's choice of the expression "ultimate reality" is in some respects unfortunate. For not only does it carry with it the suggestion of *degrees* of reality, it also suggests what he is concerned to deny, namely, that there is a world *behind* our world about which religion speaks. His point, however, seems to be that religion is concerned with what is not apparent. It is concerned, that is to say, with the terms in which human life should ultimately be understood. The question about *theism* may be put quite simply: Does talk about an ultimate reality *presuppose* a "most real thing" (*ens realissimum*)? Robinson's contention is that it does not.

He does not deny that there may have been some value in regarding 'theos' as *a Person*. But this is no more than a "human projection", to be retained in so far as it may be of value for the religious life. He does not doubt that there may be many for whom it still has the value it once had. He views the man-in-the-pew who thinks this "projection" can only be abandoned by giving up the Christian faith altogether with the same tolerance as the man-in-the-street might have expected from Berkeley for thinking that *The Principles of Human Knowledge* was a piece of anti-science.[6] But just as realism with regard to material objects might be thought less pardonable in those who,

---

[6] Berkeley's views on the Philosophy of Science were indeed very sophisticated. His short *De Motu* and his arguments towards the end of the *Principles* remain valuable contributions to that subject. He was quite emphatic that his philosophy did not undermine Physics, though he thought the claims of Physics should be interpreted in an instrumentalist manner.

like philosophers, pretend to "speak strictly", so too, it might be argued, it is less excusable for such people to take this human projection for a necessary existence.

Now Berkeley's *Principles* might have afforded some comfort to any sceptic who thought Newtonian Mechanics was founded on a wholly unwarranted assumption of the existence of material substance. In a similar way the sceptic who thinks that the Christian religion is also founded on the quite unwarranted assumption of the existence of a Highest Being might find some comfort in Robinson's *Honest to God*. For just as the notion of material substance is a way of expressing to ourselves the reality of our sense-impressions; so we may view the idea of God as a person as

> a way of making real and vivid to the imagination, by personification, the conviction that reality at its deepest level is to be interpreted not simply at the level of its impersonal, mathematical regularities but in categories like love and trust, freedom, responsibility and purpose. The real question of God is not the *existence* of a Being whom we may visualize as embodying these in his Person. It is whether this conviction about the ultimate nature of things is true (*Exploration into God*, p. 36).

Robinson, in allowing that theism may have been a legitimate *phase*[7] of Christianity, is less radical than his "Berkeleyan" thesis might suggest. In this respect Paul Tillich's attack on theism, to which Robinson acknowledges a considerable debt, is more thorough-going.

28. TILLICH'S A-THEISM

According to Tillich, ordinary theism "has made God a heavenly, completely perfect person who resides above the world and mankind". Tillich's dismissal[8] of this view is quite blunt:

[7] This is really an inconsistent concession, as a piece of theology. In his Preface to *Honest to God* (p. 10), Robinson expressed the expectation that, in retrospect, his book would be seen as having erred not in being too radical but "in not being radical enough". This concession seems to be one point where Robinson is insufficiently radical.

[8] *Systematic Theology*, Chicago (University of Chicago Press) and London (Nisbet) Vol. I 1953, p. 271. Hereinafter referred to as "ST".

"The protest of atheism against such a highest person is correct." When he says "correct" here he means "*theologically* correct". For theism has, on his view, always involved an inadequate concept of God. Thus he argues against those who have claimed a *necessary existence* for such a Being, on the strength of the Ontological Argument, in the following terms:

> Both the concept of existence and the method of arguing to a conclusion are inadequate for the idea of God. However it is defined, the "existence of God" contradicts the idea of a creative ground of essence and existence. . . . The scholastics were right when they asserted that in God there is no difference between essence and existence. But they perverted their insight when in spite of this assertion they spoke of the existence of God and tried to argue in favour of it. Actually they did not mean "existence". They meant the reality, the validity, the truth of the idea of God, an idea which did not carry the connotation of some*thing* or some*one* who might or might not exist. Yet this is the way in which the idea of God is understood today in scholarly as well as in popular discussions about the "existence of God". It would be a great victory for Christian apologetics if the words "God" and "existence" were very definitely separated except in the paradox of God becoming manifest under the conditions of existence, that is, in the Christological paradox. God does not exist. He is being-itself beyond essence and existence. Therefore, to argue that God exists is to deny him (ST I 227).

Tillich's rejection of theism does not, however, rest solely on theological grounds. He is very considerably influenced by Kant's critical philosophy. He criticizes Leibniz and Spinoza for attempting what Kant would have called a "transcendental" use of the categories 'cause' and 'substance'. God is thus made subject to what Tillich terms "the categories of finitude". In the case of Leibniz, this has the consequence of placing God too much on one side as the *cause* of finite things. In the case of Spinoza, God is made the *substance* of finite things, as a result of which He "is merged into finite beings, and their being is his being" (ST I 263). Tillich himself uses the word "ground" as what "oscillates between cause and substance and transcends both of them" (ST I 173). But when he speaks of God as "the ground of our being" he is using the word "ground" as a "symbol", not as a "category".

The theological and philosophical criticisms of theism offered by Tillich converge on the complaint that to speak of God as "existing" is to reduce him to anthropomorphic dimensions. The God of theism is characterized by Tillich[9] as

> a being besides others and as such a part of the whole of reality. He certainly is considered its most important part, but as a part and therefore as subjected to the structure of the whole. He is supposed to be beyond the ontological elements and categories which constitute reality. But every statement subjects him to them. He is seen as a self which has a world, as a ego which is related to a thou, as a cause which is separated from its effect, as having a definite space and an endless time. He is a being, not being itself.

Tillich's attempt at a non-theistic characterization of the language of religion presents many difficulties. A number of these have to do with his notion of 'being-itself'. For if the Ontological Argument has been open, in some of its traditional forms, to the criticism that it treats existence and reality as *properties* of God, Tillich's language suggests he may be open to the criticism that he treats them as *things*. "Being-itself" is "that which is not a special being or a group of beings, not something concrete or something abstract, but rather something which is always thought implicitly, and sometimes explicitly, if something is said to *be*" (ST I 181). The trouble with *theism*, according to Tillich, is that it makes God feature as only a *part* of the picture we have of reality. The trouble with Tillich's *a-theism*, on the other hand, is that it seems to identify God with the picture itself.

He comes to do this as a result of what seem to be astonishing confusions over the notions of 'form' and 'structure'. He wishes to argue for a quasi-Kantian ontology as a central part of philosophy. "Ontology is not a speculative-fantastic attempt to establish a world behind the world; it is an analysis of those structures of being which we encounter with every meeting with reality" (ST I 24). "Theology", he goes on to say, "presupposes in every sentence the structure of being, its categories, laws, and concepts." But what are those *structures of being*? They are

[9] *The Courage to Be*, London (Nisbet) and Yale (Yale University Press) 1952, p. 184.

"the general structures that make experience possible" (ST I 22).
But this is only another way of speaking about the terms in
which experience *must* be understood if it is to be possible. It is
a way of speaking about what might be called "the grammar
of experience".

But Tillich, having got hold of some notion of 'structure',
seems to have been quite carried away by it. He says that God
"is not subject to the structure", meaning that it is wrong to
try to speak of him in terms of the "categories of finitude".
But he then goes on:

> the structure is grounded in him. He *is* this structure, and it is
> impossible to speak about him except in terms of this structure.
> God must be approached cognitively through the structural
> elements of being-itself. . . . They enable us to use symbols which
> we are certain point to the ground of reality (ST I 264).

But how could God be identified with what is, after all, a
conceptual structure? The answer seems to be that it was not the
intention to identify him with a *conceptual* structure but with
the structure of being which ontological inquiry lays bare for
us.

Tillich does not only speak of God as "being-itself" or "the
structure of being". He also speaks of him as "the ground of
our being" and even the "power of being". He attempts to
link up his ontological structure with some account of creation,
providence and grace. In doing so, however, he adds to his
notion of 'structure' the connotation of 'support'. Thus: "The
faith in God's sustaining creativity is the faith in the *continuity*
of the *structure* of reality as the *basis* for being and acting"
(ST I 291, my italics). Tillich seems indeed to be a master of
the unconscious pun. For he even muddles up "structure" in
his quasi-Kantian sense already mentioned with that equivalent
to the Scholastic term "form". In this way he manages to
conjure up a connection between "the structure of being" and
"the power of being":

> Being is inseparable from the logic of being, the structure which
> makes it what it is and which gives reason the power of grasping
> and shaping it. "Being something" means having a form. . . .

Whatever loses its form loses its being. Form should not be contrasted with content. The form which makes a thing what it is, is
its content, its *essentia*, its definite power of being (ST I 197).

In this way Tillich scrambles over his hastily-erected bridge
from ontology to theology. A transition is made from the sense
of "structure" which is precisely *contrasted* with "content" to
that which has given the Cosmological Argument its perennial
appeal, which is connected with "the ground of our being".

But the bridge is not adequate to make the transition from the
basis on which Tillich's criticism of theism rests to what might
serve as a non-theistic theology. Tillich's ubiquitous notion of
'structure' is too riddled with ambiguity, not to mention
obscurity, to carry the weight of such a transition. And the
reason for his confusions over the notion does not seem far to
seek. It lies in his re-ification of the "structures . . . which are
presupposed in the cognitive encounter with every realm of
reality". It lies in his use of epistemology as a basis for ontology.

If this diagnosis of what goes wrong in Tillich's account of
the language of religion is correct, it seems as if there may still
be a great deal of value in that account. For if he is guilty of
identifying the conceptual structure in terms of which we must
understand our experience with "the structure of reality" and
further re-ifying this structure into "being-itself", some hope is
offered of re-interpreting him by reversing this process. We may,
that is to say, put a de-ontologized gloss upon his claims.
When, for example, he says: "God *is* the structure in terms of
which we should speak of him", we may re-express his claim
by saying: "The grammatical claims which articulate the
conceptual structure in terms of which religion attempts to
present an understanding of human experience are all claims
about God." Or rather—to express it more correctly—God is
what those grammatical claims are about. It does indeed make
some difference which way round the point is put. For if one
says that theology is concerned with God and his dealings with
men, this suggests that the existence of God is a presupposition
of theological inquiry. Expressed this way round, it seems open
to the unbeliever to say: Show me that this Being exists and

then I may take your subject seriously. After all, who would take ornithology seriously if there were no birds? But if one says, as Robinson does, that God is what theology is about rather than the other way around, the question about the existence of God will be seen to be reducible to the question whether it is possible to speak about the terms in which human experience should *ultimately* be understood.

That is, the *external* question, the unbeliever's question, about the existence of God will be so reducible. The *internal* question cannot be answered in wholly non-theological terms. Nor shall I be concerned to answer either question here. Rather I shall try to indicate the *meta-grammatical* nature of ontological questions, including that about the existence of God. I hope to bring out why the *external* question about the existence of God must be taken as a question about the acceptability of religion as a whole. For *its* language seems to be the only language which could *require* the existence of God. The *internal* question about the existence of God is thus a meta-grammatical one.

29. ONTOLOGY AS META-GRAMMAR

I have suggested that Tillich is misled by his understanding of ontological questions into supposing that there could be a form of inquiry into "the structure of being". But how should ontological claims, i.e. existence claims of a non-matter-of-fact character, be understood? We may approach this question by considering a radically-conventionalist account of such questions. The criticisms which I will offer will parallel, and I hope re-inforce, my earlier criticisms (see Section II) of such accounts of necessary truth.

Carnap presents[10] the problem about the nature of ontological disputes in the following terms:

> Are there properties, classes, numbers, propositions? In order to understand more clearly the nature of these and related problems,

[10] In his article "Empiricism, Semantics, and Ontology", reprinted in *Meaning and Knowledge* (ed. E. Nagel and R. B. Brandt), New York (Harcourt, Brace and World) 1965, p. 298ff.

it is above all necessary to recognize a fundamental distinction between two kinds of questions concerning the existence or reality of entities. If someone wishes to speak in his language about a new kind of entities, he has to introduce a system of new ways of speaking, subject to new rules; we shall call this procedure the construction of a linguistic *framework* for the new entities in question. And now we must distinguish between two kinds of questions of existence; first, questions of the existence of certain entities of the new kind *within the framework*; we call them *internal questions*; and second, questions concerning the existence or reality *of the system of entities as a whole*, called *external questions*. Internal questions and possible answers to them are formulated with the help of the new forms of expressions. The answers may be found either by purely logical methods or by empirical methods, depending upon whether the framework is a logical or a factual one.

He gives as an example of such a linguistic framework what he calls the "thing-language". *Within* that language one can ask such questions as "Are centaurs real or merely imaginary?" For the rules of the framework within which they are asked provide us with a means of answering them. But now, supposing someone raises the question whether there really are (material) things *at all*? This is what Carnap terms an *external question*, since it is about the "reality of the thing world itself". It is, he notes, a question which it is characteristic of the philosopher to ask:

> Realists give an affirmative answer, subjective idealists a negative one, and the controversy goes on for centuries without ever being solved. And it cannot be solved because it is framed in the wrong way. To be real in the scientific sense means to be an element of the system; hence this concept cannot be applied to the system itself. Those who raise the question of the reality of the thing world itself have perhaps in mind not a theoretical question as their formulation seems to suggest, but rather a practical question, a matter of a practical decision concerning the structure of our language. We have to make the choice whether or not to accept and use the forms of expression in the framework in question.

Carnap wishes to deny that the decision to adopt one linguistic framework rather than another can be of a "cognitive nature". He denies, in other words, that there could be any such thing as "ontological insight". There are, however, factors which may influence our decision to adopt one framework rather than another. For example, the thing language works "with a high degree of efficiency for most purposes of everyday life". We should not, however, say: "The fact of the efficiency of the thing language is confirming evidence for the reality of the thing world". We should rather say instead: "This fact makes it advisable to accept the thing language."

Tillich, by contrast, does think there can be ontological insights. For he says that the philosopher is concerned with the "structure of reality as a whole":

> He tries to penetrate into the structures of being by means of the power of his cognitive function and its structures. He assumes— and science continuously confirms this assumption—that there is an identity, or at least an analogy, between objective and subjective reason, between the *logos* of reality as a whole and the *logos* working in him. . . . There is no particular place to discover the structure of being; there is no particular place to stand to discover the categories of experience. The place to look is all places; the place to stand is no place at all; it is pure reason (ST I 27).

In engaging in "a critical analysis of experience", the philosopher may uncover "ontological concepts" which constitute the structure of experience. Those concepts are necessarily applicable to experience. The entities which come under them are necessarily to be found in reality. Pure reason can, therefore, by a critical analysis of experience, discover such entities.

In Tillich's terms, we might regard Berkeley's attempt to prove the existence of God as the attempt to establish that 'God' was an ontological concept. But, over against Tillich, it may be insisted that the most that he could have established is the necessity of the concept 'God' within a given linguistic framework. The *assumption* of a correspondence between the structure of our understanding of the world and the structure of reality cannot be made (See Section 7 above). On this point Carnap seems to be right. But, over against Carnap, it is open for us to reject the Berkeleyan linguistic framework within which the existence of such an entity is necessary. It is open for us to reject it, moreover, on other than merely pragmatic grounds. For we may claim that some of the concepts involved in this framework are inadequate. This is so, for example, with

Berkeley's concept of 'cause'. Why is that concept inadequate? Because, it might be said, it makes it a necessary matter that only an *agent* can cause something. If we reject this framework, we do so because we regard it as involving a *false* understanding of the concept 'cause'. We believe it to be true, that is to say, that something other than an agent can be a cause. Our decision not to accept that linguistic framework is, therefore, of a "cognitive nature".

The question of the existence of God, raised as an *external* question, must be construed as one which calls in question the language of religion as a whole. For the statement "God exists", if it *is* true, could only be true as a meta-grammatical statement. To reject it as false is to reject the linguistic framework which requires it to be true. Neither a religious nor a non-religious framework could make it possible to regard the existence of God as a question of fact. As an *internal* question, the question whether there is a God could only be whether a non-theistic grammar of religion is possible. But *that* question can only be raised *within* the linguistic framework of a given religion.

The ontological dispute between Berkeley's position and that of Locke may also be regarded as one about meta-grammar. The issue, that is to say, is one about what is presupposed by the language of sense-perception. On one side, it could be said, it is held that we could only speak of veridical sense-perception if there were such substances. On the other side it is claimed that it makes no sense to speak of anything existing if a mind does not perceive it. Since, therefore, material substances were admitted to be unobservable in principle, talk about them must be dismissed as unintelligible. The ontological dispute springs from a disagreement in the account given of the grammar of the language of perception. Locke holds, for example, that something may be a cause which is not an agent and that something may exist which is not actually being perceived. Neither of these claims makes sense, on Berkeley's terms.

It seems, then, that Robinson is right to construe his

non-theistic account of Christianity as analogous to Berkeley's material-substance-free account of perception. But he *ought*, it has been suggested, to be pressing the analogy more closely. He ought, that is to say, to be claiming not merely that the Christian religion does not require the supposition of a Highest Being. He ought to be maintaining that the language of the Christian religion actually *precludes* talk about such a being. This more radical claim is made by Tillich. If we may reduce Tillich's talk about "the structure of being" to talk about the grammar of the Christian religion, we may find in his *Systematic Theology* much that would count as a contribution to the development of a non-theistic grammar of Christianity.

Tillich's central pre-occupation is with the question of what concept of God is adequate, from a Christian point of view. His objection to theism is that its concept is not adequate. For it over-emphasizes one aspect of a polarity between individualization and participation, representing God as an absolute individual. Tillich denies that it is meaningful to do this. The only sense in which it *is* meaningful is that in which it is equally meaningful to talk of God as the "absolute participant". "The one term cannot be applied without the other." For "God is equally 'near' to each of them while transcending them both" (ST I 271). If we recognize this, we see how the problem of God's both being loving and just—a problem to which theism cannot give an intelligible answer—may be met. We may say:

> . . . the creature who violates the structure of justice . . . violates love itself. When this happens—and it is the character of creaturely existence that it happens universally—judgment and condemnation follow. But they do not follow by a special act of divine wrath for retribution . . . condemnation can only mean that the creature is left to the non-being it has chosen (ST I 315).

This case has been mentioned before (Section 26 above). It is a case which seems to present difficulties for theism. But it is one which only a theologian can assess. What I am saying contributes, if it contributes at all, to the theological issue indirectly. For the issue can only be discussed in a relevant way if it is first made clear what kind of issue is involved. And this is a question of what might loosely be termed the "logic" of religious discourse.

Some indication should be given, however, of what would count as a refutation of Tillich's position. It would involve showing that the language of religion could not be made intelligible without supposing there to be a Divine Person. One line of criticism might be, that it is essential to the religious life that the believer be thought of as related to God in a personal way. But how can one make sense of this, it might be asked, if God is not a Person? Surely, it will be said, it makes no sense to speak of a relation to being-itself. Tillich's way of answering this question seems to involve agreeing that one cannot speak of a relation to God as one can to a Person. But he argues that it makes no sense to suppose there could be such a relation:

> God as being-itself is the ground of every relation; in his life all relations are present beyond the distinctions between potentiality and actuality. But they are not the relations of God with something else. They are inner relations of the divine life. The internal relations are, of course, not conditioned by the actualization of finite freedom. But the question is whether there are external relations between God and the creature. The doctrine of creation affirms that God is the creative ground of everything in every moment. In this sense there is no creaturely independence from which an external relation between God and the creature could be derived (ST I 300 f.).

Tillich expresses these internal relations by speaking in terms of the "structure" of being. The theistic understanding of 'sin' as an offence against a Person is replaced by talk of a man's "violating the structure of justice". The theistic understanding of 'punishment' represents God as *free* yet in some way *bound* to punish the wicked. Tillich opposes this with an account which, since it is presented in the very language he wishes to question, has an air of deliberate paradox:

> God is called "free", but he is free not in arbitrariness but in an absolute and unconditional identity with his destiny, so that he himself is his destiny, so that the essential structures of his being are not strange to his freedom but are the actuality of his freedom (ST I 270).

The antinomies of freedom and determinism, as applied to God, show the inadequacies of treating Him as a Person. Tillich uses the language of theism in order to provide theological "insight". For to understand him is to recognize the inadequacy of the concept of God embodied in theism. He does not reject the language of theism as *such*, only the construction put on it. Personal language provides us with the language in which it is most appropriate to speak of God. But it does not follow from this that God is *a Person*. That involves taking our "symbols" too seriously, of giving them the status of categories. This view finds a clear expression in the following passage:

> If we speak, *as we must*, of the ego-thou relation between God and man, the thou embraces the ego and consequently the entire relation. If it were otherwise, if the ego-thou relation with God were *proper rather than symbolic*, the ego could withdraw from the relation. But there is no place to which man can withdraw from the divine thou, because it includes the ego and is nearer to the ego than the ego to itself. Ultimately, it is an insult to the divine holiness to talk about God as we do of objects whose existence or non-existence can be discussed (ST I 301, my italics).

Tillich's thesis, then, is that the existence of God is not a question which can meaningfully be discussed. It is, it should be stressed, a thesis advanced about and in the language of the Christian religion. He is not saying that there cannot be monotheistic religion. On the contrary, he discusses four forms which it may take (ST I 250ff.). He admits that Christianity, particularly in its liturgy, has often presented God as "a monarch who rules over heavenly beings, angels, and spirits", as "the Lord of Hosts". But that involves an inadequate understanding of the concept 'God', according to Tillich.

The question about the existence of God, like any ontological question, can only be raised within a given language. It can, therefore, only be construed as a question about meta-grammar, about what is presupposed by the acceptance of certain grammatical claims. Berkeley's attempted proof of the existence of God illustrates the attempt of some traditional apologetics to base a meta-grammatical claim that God must exist upon non-religious grammatical claims. I do not wish here to presume upon the failure of such attempts. On the other hand, they have little bearing on the question of the existence of the God of, say, the Christian religion. The resolution of one such meta-grammatical question is independent of that which may be appropriate to the other. It remains as open to theologians to object that Tillich's concept of God is inadequate as it is for philosophers to object to Berkeley's concept of a 'sensible thing'. But it is no more pertinent to criticize Tillich without regard to the language of the Christian religion than it would be to attack Berkeley's account of perception on, say, theological grounds. The problem about raising the theistic question without regard to the language of any religion is that it leaves the prior question about what concept of God would be an adequate one in a vacuum.

It should be mentioned that the criticism I offered of Malcolm (Section 27) is deficient in just this respect. For it was essential to this criticism to insist that it is a requirement of ascribing omnipotence to any being that it should exist, if it exists, as a contingent matter of fact. Malcolm himself notes that it would follow from such an account of the nature of the deity that it would make sense to ask questions like the following: "Will God still exist next week?" or "He was in existence yesterday but how about today?" But he thinks it is absurd to make God the subject of such questions. For "according to our ordinary conception of Him" God is an *eternal* being. And to say that God is "eternal" is to say that any statement (or question) about him which implied that he has *duration* would be senseless.

The merit, however, of this conception of the deity—be it ordinary or otherwise—depends on considerations of a theological character. The claim that God is an eternal being is grammatical in character. Whether or not it is true that a grammatical mistake is made by someone who speaks as if God were a being having endless duration depends upon the "conventions" governing the language in which he is speaking. Whether or not the claim itself can be said to be true depends on whether or not the conception of God as an "eternal" being is an adequate one. And that question—like the question whether the conception of God as "a being" is an adequate one—can only be decided within the context of a particular religion. To allow a defence of Malcolm by saying that it makes no sense to apply temporal predicates to God would be to make a theological concession. An argument which requires such a concession must be deficient in so far as it is not reasonable to demand it.

One reason for not making such a concession is that it is not clear just how much would be conceded in making it. For the point of distinguishing between eternity and endless duration is itself religious. And those who do not see the point will not have the notion of eternity made intelligible for them by being told what it is *not*. It remains, despite Malcolm's explanation, unclear what can be meant by speaking of a *being* to whom temporal predicates cannot significantly be applied. It is therefore unclear whether or not one would be talking nonsense in ascribing to such a being the performance of actions which, when performed by other beings, are thought of as involving temporal predicates. To the extent indeed that it is not clear what would be meant by speaking of God as both omnipotent *and* "eternal" it is not clear what conception of God is taken by Malcolm as the starting-point of his argument.

Certain grammatical assumptions are made by all the theistic arguments. These are not, except in the case of the Ontological Argument, assumptions about the nature of the deity. But in this case they are theological in character. The vagueness of expressions like "the most *perfect* being" and "that than which a *greater* cannot be thought" help to disguise the fact that the acceptance of a particular religious tradition is being relied upon. Malcolm's form of the argument involves him in being more specific about his premisses. But to that extent he seems more firmly committed to a theological starting-point.

X

THE INTELLIGIBILITY GAP

THE ARGUMENT of this essay has been directed towards showing that there is a form of B-thesis which may correctly account for the intelligibility gap between believer and unbeliever. In support of such an account an attempt has been made to establish a legitimate class of claims of which it could be said that one cannot understand them without believing them to be true. Some notion of insight, it has been suggested, is needed to account for the possibility of any intelligibility gap being bridged. So far this notion has been treated in somewhat general and informal terms. The reader's attention has been directed to examples for an explanation of it. It is now time to treat of insight in a more systematic manner.

30. THE STRUCTURE OF INSIGHT

An expression of insight has been represented as standing, as it were, on the watershed between two different ways of understanding something. Seen from one side it can only appear as unintelligible. Yet looked at from the other side its truth can be recognized. The possibility of moving from one view of it to the other is due, it has been said, to conceptual change. A general characterization of 'insight' must necessarily be a vague one. For changes in the grammatical standing of a claim cover a range of cases. A more specific account of the concept will need to mention the kinds of case which there may be.

There are, in the first place, those cases where the expression of insight comes to be regarded as *necessarily* true or false where the claim in question had formerly been regarded as only *contingently* true or false. Then there are those cases where the change is the other way around, where what has been regarded as necessary comes to be thought of as only contingently true or false. With each of these cases we may distinguish between those cases where the truth-value is retained and those where it is not. Finally, there is the case where what was formerly regarded as necessarily false comes to be regarded as necessarily true. These five kinds of case may all be seen to involve conceptual change. They may thus be distinguished sharply from the change involved in coming to regard as contingently false what one had formerly thought of as contingently true, or vice-versa.

These five kinds of case may be brought out by reference to examples already given:

(i) An example of change from regarding a claim as contingently true to thinking of it as necessarily true was mentioned in Section 26. On one kind of understanding of God as a super-human individual it becomes a contingent matter that the wicked are punished, even though it is believed that they are invariably punished. But, as understood by Kierkegaard and Tillich, the connection between being wicked and being "punished" is represented as an internal one. It is, that is to say, a connection which is expressed by a grammatical claim. The change is prompted by a concern for a more adequate concept of God. To accept it is to accept an insight into the nature of divine judgment.

(ii) A number of examples have been given where a conceptual change involves something being regarded as necessarily true which had formerly been seen as contingently false. This status might be accorded to Berkeley's *esse est percipi* principle. For it has generally been thought to be false, as a matter of fact, that anything which exists is always actually being perceived by some person. Yet, on Berkeley's view, it would make no sense to say of something which was other than a spirit that it *existed* if it was not actually being perceived. Whether or not Berkeley's concept of existence is really more adequate than that which is commonly accepted depends very largely on the adequacy of his account of perception.

Among the religious examples mentioned which fall into this category are: Barth's claim that "A man who believes once believes once for all" (Section 25), Feuerbach's claim that the human race, taken as a whole, must be perfect (Section 5) and Kierkegaard's claim that the lover is not forgotten (Section 26). Each of these presents as necessarily true what would commonly be regarded as contingently false. Barth and Kierkegaard may be taken as offering insights into the concepts of 'faith' and 'love' respectively. Feuerbach's claim might be similarly understood with regard to the concept 'species'. But his concept of 'species' arises out of his attempt to connect a man's understanding with his nature such that it would make no sense for a *man* to suppose that there could be a higher nature than his own.

(iii) Examples mentioned where the change is from a claim's being necessarily true to contingently false include the claim that the Moon is perfectly spherical and that the Earth cannot influence the Moon (Section 11). The case of hypocrisy (Section 12) is one where a claim regarded as necessarily true (i.e. that the hypocrite regards himself as insincere) is seen as being sometimes true and sometimes false, i.e. as contingently true or false.

(iv) The only case I have cited where the change in status from necessary to contingent preserves truth-value is in Section 18. It is that of a man who comes to recognize that it would make sense to suppose that there were events which lacked natural causes but believes that, as a matter of fact, there never have and never will be such events. He abandons his belief that every event has a natural cause as a *grammatical* proposition but holds it to be true still, only true as a generalization.

(v) A conceptual change must be involved when an expression of insight represents as necessarily true what has been regarded as necessarily false, or *vice versa*. It could be said that, whereas for Locke it was a matter of grammar that there had to be material substances if veridical perception was to be possible, it was equally a matter of grammar for Berkeley that there could not be such substances.

One religious example which has been discussed is the claim that there is no Highest Being (Section 27). Tillich's claim "God does not exist . . . he is above and beyond existence" makes no sense *in terms of the language of theism*. For how could God be understood except as a Being and how could a Being (with or without a capital "B") be intelligibly said to be "above and beyond existence"? It is tempting to dismiss such talk as absurd. But if Tillich's a-theism is seen as grammatical in character we should not be inclined to dismiss it too hastily. For, to the extent that Tillich is offering an improvement on the theistic concept of God, such a claim may turn out to express a theological insight. Whether or not it does so is a matter for theology to decide.

It is not important to the argument of this essay that any of these examples should actually be cases of insights. It is sufficient that they should have been thought to be such. There is indeed no general recipe for deciding whether or not a proposed conceptual change does advance understanding of a particular matter. Hence there can be no general theory for distinguishing genuine from unwarranted claims to insight. This does not mean at all that there is no distinction to be made. But the distinction can only be made by reference to the particulars of a given case. The question whether Hume, in rejecting the possibility of necessary connections between events (see Section 2), provided a more adequate concept of cause has no bearing whatever on the question whether a more adequate concept of hypocrisy is gained by allowing that the hypocrite may think himself sincere. The most that expressions of insight have in common is a structure of relations to different ways of understanding some matter. But that they have in common with unwarranted claims to insight.

31. RELIGIOUS AND EVERYDAY LANGUAGE

It has been claimed, at the end of Chapter VII, that if a B-thesis can be sustained over against an S-thesis with regard to a given religion, then the *distinctiveness* of the language of that religion must be conceded. It must, that is to say, be conceded that the norms of intelligibility which govern discourse in that religion are to be found implicit in that discourse. It may, however, appear that such autonomy could only be secured at the price of divorcing the language of religion from that in terms of which men otherwise understand their experience. Uncompromisingly theological versions of the B-thesis, such as that put forward by Barth, seem particularly liable to this objection. Yet it seems that religion could only be related satisfactorily to everyday life if the language of religion was related in some way to everyday language. What is at stake here is not, or not primarily, the viability of a programme of apologetics but the possibility of genuine religion. For if religion is concerned with providing the terms in which human experience should *ultimately* be understood, the idea of a religion unconnected with everyday life could only be a decadent one. A religious understanding must be internally connected with a religious way of life in that to understand the meaning of human life in a religious way is to see the possibility of its being lived in a particular way.

It is possible, however, to reconcile insistence on the autonomy of theology with the requirement that the language of religion should be related to that of everyday life. It is only if, as is claimed by advocates of the D-thesis, that relation must consist in expressing religious claims as claims intelligible within everyday language that the autonomy of the language of religion is in jeopardy. The account given by a B-thesis of the relation of religious to everyday language must not subject religious claims to the norms implicit in everyday language. Yet it must make clear what relation obtains between religious and everyday language. These conditions are met if it is said that religious *insights* may be expressed in everyday language. For, in so far as they purport to be insights, they must be regarded as possibly being subject to other norms of intelligibility than those to which they may appear (by virtue of the language in which they are couched) to be subject. They must, that is to say, be regarded as introducing a change in those concepts to which they refer. A religious understanding is related to that understanding implicit in our use of everyday language in that it purports to transform it. In doing so it introduces new, allegedly more adequate, concepts. It is the nature of and connection between those concepts which becomes the subject-matter of theology. That is the sense in which I have described theology as "grammar".

Since one cannot always readily distinguish between a genuine insight and a spurious claim to one without further study, one ought not to be too hasty in dismissing what appears on the face of it to be unintelligible. The temptation to lump religion and superstition together may arise, in part, from the kind of impatience which prompts the conventionalist move against claims which violate the norms which govern ordinary discourse. When it is said, for example, that virtue *is* its own reward, it is tempting to dismiss what is said as nonsense. For, we may reason, how *could* the reward itself be identical with that which earns it? In terms of the language in which we speak of rewards it *is* nonsense to claim that virtue is its own reward. But the "nonsense" has its point, namely, of calling in question the way in which we commonly understand virtue and vice. If one had an adequate concept of virtue, it might be argued, one would see that it made no sense to ask whether the virtuous life "paid off". One way of expressing this putative insight in relation to the common belief that the point virtue has is as a means to some desired end is to say "Virtue *is* its own reward".

I do not think it could be maintained that this claim to insight is *spurious*. For it does seem to introduce us, or attempt to introduce us, to a different concept of virtue. But one is not obliged, in accepting that such a claim to insight is *not* spurious, to admit that it is a genuine insight. It is possible to reject the proposed conceptual change on precisely the grounds that it is advocated. It is possible, that is to say, to deny what is implicit in any claim to insight, namely, that the concept being introduced is more adequate than that already available. This will involve rejecting the concept as unintelligible. But it is nevertheless possible to have some grasp of the concept on which one may rely in rejecting it. The background commonly present to any claim to insight both makes it possible to see that a distinctive concept is being introduced and provides some basis for acceptance or rejection of the concept.

Now if religious claims are designed to transform our understanding of experience, there is some case for saying, as is sometimes said, that the words which we use in speaking of God have a different sense when applied to him from the sense which they ordinarily have. We have already seen how the meaning of the word "judge" is changed when it is applied to God. But this is because a different concept of judgment is introduced from that which we commonly share (See Section 26 above). Hence it is not only what is said *about God* which is affected, but also what is said, by the believer, about other matters. His understanding of what it is for God to be a judge affects his understanding of what it is to pass judgment on another man. Kierkegaard[1] went so far as to claim that it was impossible for us to have the kind of ethical detachment which would make it possible for us to judge others ethically. For, he argues, "the ethical, as being the internal, cannot be observed by an outsider". Ethical reality cannot be known by mere thought, since it is "the individual's own reality". One can only apprehend the ethical reality of another person by thinking it. But in so thinking it, one is thinking of that person only as a possibility.

Having provided the background which is here only hinted at, Kierkegaard goes on to speak about what is involved in judging others ethically. He writes:

> The Scriptures teach: "Judge not, that ye be not judged." This is expressed in the form of a warning, an admonition, but it is at the same time an impossibility. One human being cannot judge another ethically, because he cannot understand him except as a possibility. When therefore anyone attempts to judge another, the expression for his impotence is that he merely judges himself.

The object of the background provided by Kierkegaard is to bring his reader to a recognition of a respect in which the

[1] See his *Concluding Unscientific Postscript*. The quotations here made are from *A Kierkegaard Anthology* (ed. R. Bretall), OUP. 1947, p. 226f. in the translation by D. F. & L. M. Swenson and W. Lowrie.

concept of a moral judgment reflected in common language is less than adequate. For according to that concept of moral judgment, one clearly *can* pass moral judgments on others without necessarily, in so doing, standing condemned oneself.

Whether or not Kierkegaard's account does provide us with insight into what it is for a man to attempt to judge another ethically is too large a question to enter into here. For it is closely connected with his difficult and easily misunderstood view that truth is "subjectivity". Be it unwarranted or genuine, however, this case well exemplifies the relation between the language of religion and common language. For Kierkegaard's claim is not intelligible in accordance with the grammar which commonly governs the terms in which it is expressed. The point of so expressing it is to change that grammar—to transform that understanding of moral judgment implicit in the language we have learned to use.

In suggesting that it is a feature of the gap between believer and non-believer that such religious claims as may be expressed in everyday language do not make sense by the standards implicit in that language, the argument of this essay is exposed to the objection that it tends to support an excessively prophetic view of religion. The religious teacher, on such a view, would need to be recalling the believers perpetually from that false understanding of human experience which is inculcated by the language and way of life which they share with society at large. But how far is such a view acceptable?

It may indeed be said of some religions, e.g. the Semitic religions, that they are prophetic in just this way. They recognize that the religious way of life needs to be guarded against heresy, superstition, idolatry and other sources of corruption. This is not to say there has never been indifference or apathy about such matters. But these religions provide room for someone to draw attention to any decline in what is regarded as "true religion"—and to do it "in the name of God". And this would not be possible if the language of religion were not independent of that of the society in which it is placed.

Religions like Christianity and Islam retain this prophetic

character no less in countries where they are firmly established. But there are religions which lack any counter-part to what these religions understand by a "man of faith". They make no distinction between the believer and any other member of the society in whose way of life the practices of such a religion are entangled. But if there is no tension at any time between a religion and a given society, there are factors, such as social change, which would tend to promote such tension. For then those who accept it will be confronted with alternative beliefs and practices which may not be acceptable, e.g. if such social changes bring about wide-spread secularization. In so far as the need to correct the effects of such a change is felt, it will manifest itself by a tendency to express religious belief in opposition to that which it seeks to correct. The form such expression takes will be what is here called "insight". For the opposition could not be over issues which are matters of fact. It is, rather, conceptual in character.

More needs to be said, however, to do justice to the *dependence* of the language of religion upon that of common life. For it is not enough to say that religion is concerned to transform that understanding of human experience which is implicit in common language. It is often the case that, in learning everyday language, we do not acquire any understanding to which religion stands clearly opposed. Sometimes we learn language in such a way that our grammar precludes as unintelligible certain religious questions about understanding rather than provides us with an alternative understanding. We may be so placed, for example, with regard to questions like "What is the *meaning* of human life?" If, on the other hand, our upbringing has been a religious one, our grammar may admit such questions.

This suggests that there is an a-symmetry between the expression of religious and of anti-religious insights. The man who, like Feuerbach, claims to "see through" religion has to express himself *both* in relation to the language of religion *and* in relation to the language in terms of which alleged religious insights are expressed. When, for example, Feuerbach claims that the truth which finds its distorted expression in the Doctrine of the Trinity is that there is a "universal significance" in the relations between individuals, he both rejects the religious and commends a humanitarian understanding of those relations (See Section 5). Feuerbach himself supposes that he is doing no more than bringing out what, but for religion, would be apparent anyway. But it seems rather that he is offering an understanding of human relations which is an alternative to that offered by religion. For, instead of saying "Inasmuch as you have done it to the least of these my brothers you have done it to God" he would say you have done it to the "species". His morality is equally concerned to direct attention to what is not apparent.

It seems, then, only partially true to say that there is an opposition between what can be said in religion and what can commonly be said. For religion is concerned to affect human understanding of, for example, birth, marriage and death. Religion is not practised in a vacuum but in the context of common life. To that extent there is a dependence of religious language upon the language of common life. And this dependence marks an a-symmetrical feature of the relation between them. To understand a religion is, amongst other things, to understand how it addresses itself to "the human condition". This is not to say that "the human condition" is a *datum* variously explained by different religions. For religions differ in what they take that condition to be. To allow that religious language is inconceivable without common language is not to allow that it must be understood in terms of common language.

32. CONCLUDING REMARKS

The question to which this essay has been addressed is whether religious claims can be said to make sense. It has been argued that there is no basis for a general negative or a general affirmative to this question. If, however, a general negative may be ruled out, then some account is required of how it is possible for some people to make sense of such claims whereas others do not. I have been concerned to explore the implications of saying that it is in some way a necessary matter that the non-believer should find the claims of religion unintelligible.

No conclusion follows from the arguments offered as to whether or not there is anything to learn from this or that religion. It does not follow from its being correct to hold a B-thesis with regard to a given religion that a more adequate understanding is provided by that religion than would other-wise be available to us. I have thus left open what many would regard as the crucial question about religion. My argument has been that, *so far as epistemology is concerned*, this question *should* be left open. If the form of B-thesis I have put forward is tenable, it may serve as a wedge for keeping it open.

INDEX OF NAMES

INDEX OF SUBJECTS

Major references to a topic are indicated by **bold** type